THIS I
KNOW

THIS I
KNOW

LOREN C. DUNN

Bookcraft
Salt Lake City, Utah

Library of Congress Catalog Card Number: 85-72791

ISBN 0-88494-579-0

First Printing, 1985

Printed in the United States of America

Contents

PART V.   TO ALL NATIONS

Preface

This compilation of talks was suggested by Bookcraft. I have appreciated the help and assistance of many, including Marvin Wallin, Cory Maxwell, and George Bickerstaff as they guided this work to final publication.

This I Know is a reflection of my faith in and understanding of the gospel of Jesus Christ. The writings show the influence of family and extended family, and the inspiration gained from my associates of the General Authorities and from so many faithful members of the Church over the years.

This is not an official publication of The Church of Jesus Christ of Latter-day Saints, and I alone am responsible for its content.

I.
Cultivating
The Spiritual

The power, vitality, and truth of the gospel of Jesus Christ is revealed in the spiritual gifts found within the Church. More specifically, such truth is embodied in individual and personal testimony—the greatest spiritual blessing of all. For this reason, an individual testimony must be cultivated by each member.

Learning to Live by the Spirit

The most important experience a person can have is to be influenced by the spirit of the Holy Ghost. It brings the knowledge that Jesus is the Christ. It settles once and for all any question about the truthfulness of this work. It speaks peace to the soul. It gives life direction and meaning. It heals. To live so as to receive it is to be a partaker of the greatest gift of God. "For the kingdom of God is not in word [alone], but in power" (1 Corinthians 4:20).

Some years ago a young man who was brought up in the Church left home to attend a prominent university. His interest was philosophy, and it wasn't long before he didn't know what was true and what wasn't true. He reached a point where he doubted himself and wasn't even sure if he had a testimony, and was contemplating leaving the Church.

A friend of mine, who had received a doctorate in philosophy from an eastern university, was called in to see if he could help. They sat down and chatted together; then my friend asked this young man a series of questions to see if he had had any spiritual experiences in his life. He asked questions like, "Have you ever had an answer to your prayers? Have you seen someone healed by the power of the priesthood?" And this boy had to answer no in every case, except for maybe in one or two instances. Then my friend looked at this young man and said, "How can you leave the Church when you haven't been in it yet?"

Remarks given at the Salt Lake Institute February 1974.

I think that was a very insightful comment. The power, vitality, and truth of the gospel of Jesus Christ is revealed in the spiritual gifts found within the Church. More specifically, such truth is embodied in individual and personal testimony—the greatest spiritual blessing of all. For this reason, an individual testimony *must* be cultivated by each member.

We are going through trying times; there is much upheaval and change. The people who will be able to meet these challenges will be those who are sustained by individual testimony. Gaining such a testimony is a matter of cultivating the gifts and blessings of the Spirit each day. It is an experience in communication, and it is as real as anything can be. In fact, it is more real than anything the world has to offer.

Having been educated in the communications business, I know how inappropriate and inaccurate words can be—unless the people who are talking to each other have had exactly the same experience. You can't communicate a pure thought by words alone, because the other person will interpret those words in terms of his own experience and understanding, which is never the same as yours. At its very best communication is an impure and imperfect science. But when something is conveyed to you by the power and Spirit of God, when you know something within your soul, then you begin to approach the purest kind of communication, and you can know things as they really are. We need to know that we are in the Lord's Church and that we are enjoying some of the spiritual blessings associated with that membership. We need to cultivate the Spirit of God in our lives, and we need to keep it there.

The Lord gives us this promise in section 93 of the Doctrine and Covenants:

> Verily, thus saith the Lord: It shall come to pass that every soul who forsaketh his sins and cometh unto me, and calleth on my name, and obeyeth my voice, and keepeth my commandments, shall see my face and know that I am (D&C 93:1).

The purpose of the Church is to prepare people to return ultimately to the presence of the Father and the Son. By the power of the Spirit a person can prepare his life for that marvelous experience.

One part of that admonition that is particularly interesting to me is the Lord's description of those whom he will accept as being souls who "obeyeth my voice and keepeth my commandments." One might think that those two actions are the same, but that is not necessarily so. We keep His commandments by following what has been written, and we obey His voice by following His servants and listening to that still, small voice within. Some who have transgressed will say, "I really didn't know it was wrong until someone told me." But this is not always true. There are some who would say with Amulek, "I knew . . . yet I would not know" (Alma 10:6). The Lord makes it clear in scripture that He illuminates every soul with His Spirit (see Moroni 7:16). Within ourselves we know instinctively what is right or wrong.

For those of us who have had conferred upon us the Holy Ghost, cultivating that Spirit and voice can create some very positive experiences and can draw us closer to the Lord. For example, a certain inclination or feeling to do or *not* to do something is often the Lord trying to get through to us. If we listen and follow those promptings we will learn from those experiences and He will give us additional promptings. These impressions will always be in harmony with the scriptures and the inspired guidance of Church leaders. As we become more familiar with them, ultimately we will learn to live by the Spirit.

If you reason yourself out of a spiritual communication, you make it difficult for the Lord to communicate with you. If He can't get through to you, then perhaps the promptings won't be as regular or continuous as they could be. These are promptings to your heart, and there's not a soul who is a member of the Church of Jesus Christ (and some who are not) who has not at one time or another had such promptings. Cultivate the Lord's revelations to your heart, and encourage the Spirit to help you obey His voice (see D&C 6:15). That's the purest thing you can do as far as the gospel of Jesus Christ is concerned. As a person does so, he learns to live by the Spirit; otherwise difficult decisions become relatively easy—not completely easy, but easier because he has cultivated an inclination and feeling, which is the Spirit of the Lord. Influenced by the Spirit, a person by habit and by inclination knows almost instantaneously the right decision to make and the right direction in which to go (see D&C 6:14).

There is much that we must do to prepare ourselves for that communication. We must read the scriptures; we must seek the will of the Lord; we must listen to our leaders; and we must learn to be obedient, though sometimes that's very difficult. The Lord requires the strictest obedience.

I was recently listening to a taped recording of the Doctrine and Covenants, section 93, in which the Lord again emphasized obedience as a requirement for attaining the celestial kingdom. We *must* learn to obey. This is a different obedience than that required by the military. The military requires you to act in a certain way, and if you don't want to obey, the consequences are bad enough that you do what is required of you anyway. In the gospel of Jesus Christ, we have to cause ourselves to be obedient, because no one will force us; we have to discipline ourselves so that we can follow the Lord's path. When the Lord said, "Strait is the gate, and narrow is the way, which leadeth unto [eternal] life, and few there be that find it" (Matthew 7:14), He made a literal statement. It requires obedience to be saved—and it is the kind of obedience that we need to offer of ourselves. It is not something that someone makes us do, but something that we have to do ourselves. It is born of His love for us and our love for Him (see D&C 64:34).

Some young people go through a stage of rebellion, which takes them into some very unfortunate paths before they realize that obedience is the only path that will bring ultimate peace and happiness. It's a wonderful thing when a person comes to this realization and begins to put his life in order. And it's even better when a young person can learn that lesson in advance, without having to suffer as he "kicks against the pricks," as the scriptures say, and hurts himself until he comes to realize that the best path is one of truth and righteousness.

Cultivating the Spirit of the Lord helps us to establish our own testimony, and helps us to be in a position to make our own decisions. It gives us an avenue of revelation to help govern our lives.

Look at the prophet and other leaders of the Church, and you will see men who have spent their lives putting themselves in tune with that Spirit. It doesn't happen overnight. Sometimes young people will come to Church leaders and say, "Give us your formula for success." In the anxiety of youth, they want Rule A, B, C, and D to follow so they can be like Church leaders, without realizing that it took a lifetime for these leaders to become as they are today. Desiring to cultivate the Spirit is not enough, just as keeping the commandments alone is not enough; it takes the passage of time as well—building spiritual communication into our lives and nurturing it over a period of time. It takes time to overcome. It takes time to cultivate the Spirit of the Lord and to live so as to keep that Spirit always (see D&C 50:34).

We feel our best and have the greatest peace in our lives when we feel in tune with the Spirit. This is a very real experience in the gospel of Jesus Christ. When we do feel in tune, our problems don't get any easier, but our ability to cope with them becomes infinitely greater. At the center of our efforts is our cultivation of the Spirit. The key to success in the gospel of Jesus Christ is to get the spirit of testimony and to live by it. If we can do that, we will enjoy a closeness with the Father and the Son that will enlighten us and heal us (see D&C 88:63). A testimony is what we feel when the promptings of the Holy Ghost tell us in our heart that the Church is true. Cultivating the Spirit is keeping the influence of the Holy Ghost alive in our lives and living by its impressions from day to day.

I have heard President Marion G. Romney define the spirit of testimony as something that would make you want to live the gospel even if you were on a desert island all by yourself. It's knowing that God is there, that the work is true, and that no matter where you are or in what circumstances you might be, you ought to keep the commandments and stay in harmony with the living God.

It's not just knowing, but it's doing. And it's doing under every set of circumstances (see Mosiah 18:9).

Brigham Young, speaking about this whole concept of cultivating the Spirit, made this statement:

> It was asked me by a gentleman how I guided the people by revelation. I teach them to live so that the Spirit of revelation may make plain to them their duty day by day that they are able to

guide themselves. To get this revelation it is necessary that the people live so that their spirits are as pure and clean as a piece of blank paper that lies on the desk before the inditer, ready to receive any mark the writer may make upon it. When you see the Latter-day Saints greedy, and covetous of the things of this world, do you think their minds are in a fit condition to be written upon by the pen of revelation? When people live so that the Spirit of revelation will be with them day by day, they are then in the path of their duty; if they do not live according to this rule, they live beneath their duty and privileges. I hope and pray that we may all live up to our privileges. (*Journal of Discourses*, 11:240–41.)

After Brigham Young became President of the Church, he received a revelation—a dream in which he visited the Prophet Joseph Smith. This is the advice that the Prophet Joseph gave him:

Joseph stepped toward me, and looking very earnestly yet pleasantly, said, "Tell the people to be humble and faithful, and be sure to keep the spirit of the Lord and it will lead them right. Be careful and not turn away the small still voice; it will teach you what to do and where to go; it will yield the fruits of the kingdom. Tell the brethren to keep their hearts open to conviction so that when the Holy Ghost comes to them, their hearts will be ready to receive it. They can tell the Spirit of the Lord from all other spirits; it will whisper peace and joy to their souls; it will take malice, hatred, strife and all evil from their hearts; and their whole desire will be to do good, bring forth righteousness and build up the kingdom of God. Tell the brethren that if they will follow the Spirit of the Lord they will go right. Be sure to tell the people to keep the Spirit of the Lord; and if they will, they will find themselves just as they were organized by our Father in heaven before they came into the world. Our Father in Heaven organized the human family, but they are all disorganized and in great confusion. (*Manuscript History of Brigham Young, 1846–1847, pub. by Elden Jay Watson* [Salt Lake City, 1971], pp. 529–30.)

Cultivate the Spirit of the Lord. Keep your hearts open to conviction.

A friend and I were talking about one of the great agnostics of the day and supposing what would happen if the Lord sent an angel to him. The conversation might begin something like this:

"I am an angel of the Lord."

The agnostic would say, "Oh no, you're not." You see, he is already committed to something that would keep him from accepting the truth.

Let us keep our hearts and our minds open so that the revelations of God can be written on our souls, which is a promise and a right by heritage for those who have accepted baptism and enjoy the blessing of the gospel of Jesus Christ. Let us then cultivate the Spirit of God.

How do we do it?

We do it by repentance—a beautiful principle within everyone's reach. There is only one thing worse than sin, and that is when a person fails to repent. The Book of Mormon records that the Lord became angry with His people, not only because they sinned, but because they had failed to repent. There is nothing that we cannot overcome, and there is very little that we can't be forgiven of provided we repent.

If you insist on carrying the hell and pain of unforgiven sin on your back until it drives you into the ground and makes you cynical and bitter, then I suppose that's your privilege. But you cannot at the same time enjoy the Spirit of God. If you want the Spirit of the Lord you must first repent, which means you must cease doing that which is wrong, put yourselves in an atmosphere where you will not be tempted again, ask forgiveness of the Lord, and make restitution as much as possible.

One great tragedy of moral sin is that at the point of restitution all you can really say is, "I'm sorry." You can't change what has happened; but you can say, "I'm sorry," and truly feel sorry.

If your sin is serious enough, then the Lord has said that you need to go see your bishop. That is what he is for. He is not just "my neighbor, Bill Jones." He is your bishop. The Lord has called him as such, looked on him with favor, and raised him up, not to forgive you of your sins (only the Lord can do that), but to help you and to clear you for future activity in the Church. Again, if the sin is serious enough, you need to see your bishop. If there is a question in your mind, go see your bishop anyway. He will treat it confidentially, but when you come away from that interview you will know where you stand.

Having taken these steps, you can be in a better spirit and

atmosphere and condition to enjoy the spirit of revelation, the spirit of testimony, the Spirit of Christ in your heart. Your next step is probably the hardest of all for some people, and that is to forgive yourself. It is tragic when people carry throughout their adult life the memory and guilt of sins already repented of. If you have the problem of not being able to forgive yourself after repentance, the Lord will help you if you will pray for it. Learn to forgive yourself and others, and pray that the Lord will cleanse your soul and help you forget so that you can carry on with the things that you need to do.

One of the most beautiful statements in my recollection was made by the Prophet Joseph Smith as he was going to his death. After having undergone more persecution, I suspect, than most souls on the face of this earth, with the exception of the Savior and possibly Job, still he said, ''I have a conscience void of offense toward all men.'' Here was truly a great prophet.

And yet Joseph, too, had need of repentance. If you don't think that was the case read sections 64 and 20 of the Doctrine and Covenants and other instances in which the Lord called him to repentance. As great a man as Joseph Smith was, that gives us some hope, doesn't it?

When we can repent, when we can take the necessary steps, then we begin to become like the piece of paper Brigham Young spoke of, and the Lord can begin to write on our souls and on our hearts. I promise you that He will. Indeed, He is probably already doing so; but sometimes we have so many other things being written on that paper at the same time that we can't really distinguish what He is trying to tell us.

Another requirement of fruitful spiritual communication is earnest, sincere, solemn prayer. Bishop H. Burke Peterson suggested, in an October 1973 conference address, the idea of going into your closet, or your room, or some other place where you can be alone. This should be some place to lock the door and get on your knees, wait a minute, and visualize the Father in your mind. Concentrate all your thoughts on Him, and then begin to pray to Him. He knows what you need and what you are thankful for, but the Savior has told us that you should say it anyway. So say it, and say it all. Begin to establish that openness. That kind of experience will give you the strength and peace you just can't find anywhere else; it will lift you. The person who knows how to retreat to his testimony of the Lord in this way has a great source of strength—the world will not overcome him.

Finally, I express my testimony that a person can cultivate the Spirit of God daily by reading the Book of Mormon. I know this from personal experience. If you want to get close to the Lord, if you want to get close to that Spirit, if you want to have the kinds of spiritual experiences that we have been talking about (and every member of the Church has a right to them), then I would suggest that you make this the pattern of your life— in addition to prayer and repentance, read a chapter or two or three from the Book of Mormon each day. Read them out loud. I don't know why, but it is important to me to not only read the words, but also to hear them. That book has come from God, and the Spirit of God will attend you as you read it. Little by little, that Spirit will begin to change your life in a way that you would like it changed, and some significant things will happen to you. The Prophet Joseph Smith said that the Book of Mormon was the most correct book of any on earth, and the keystone of our religion, and that a man would get nearer to God by abiding by its precepts than by any other book. That's a significant statement.

Do you want to get nearer to the Lord? There's the bridge—one that will lead you to the feet of the Savior and help establish the spirit of testimony in a most beautiful way.

In conclusion let me share some wise counsel from President Marion G. Romney:

> I urge you to get acquainted with this great book [speaking of the Book of Mormon]. Read it to your children. They are *not* too young to understand it. I remember reading it with one of my lads when he was young. On one occasion I lay in the lower bunk and he in the upper bunk. We were reading aloud alternate paragraphs of those last three marvelous chapters of Second Nephi. I heard his voice breaking and thought he had a cold, but we went on to the end of the three chapters. As we finished he said to me, "Daddy, do you ever cry when you read the Book of Mormon?"
>
> "Yes, son," I answered. "Sometimes the Spirit of the Lord serves witness to my soul that the book is true, and I do cry."

"Well," he said, "That's what happened to me tonight."

I know not all of them will respond like that, but I know some of them will. And I tell you this book was given to us of God to read and to live by, and it will hold us as close to the Spirit of the Lord as anything I know. Won't you please read it? Won't you please read it? (Conference Report, April 1949.)

May the Lord bless us. May we cultivate spirituality in our lives. May the Spirit of God be our companion, and may we begin to live so that He can guide us. May we enjoy the spiritual blessings and the spiritual peace of the gospel of Jesus Christ, which is our right to enjoy, and may we begin to draw close to Him by following those points that we have discussed.

The Lord bless you; the Lord bless us all; we all need it. We're all fighting the battle, all going through life, overcoming the problems, facing the difficulties--each in our own realm, each in our own way. Every person has his own cross, and with the help of the Lord he will be able to bear it.

I bear you my witness that this is the Church of Jesus Christ. I *know* God lives. Jesus is the Christ. Joseph Smith saw what he said he saw. Spencer W. Kimball is the prophet of the living God today. This is the Church of Jesus Christ, and let me assure you that He leads His own Church. I bear you this witness, and urge you to look into your heart and see if you don't recognize some of the fruits of the gospel of Jesus Christ, which are the spiritual blessings of this gospel. They are available to all who strive to live by the Spirit.

Building Bridges to Faith

Faith is more than just an abstract principle. It is the key to unlocking the powers of heaven. It is both a gift from God and a quality to be cultivated. As we develop faith by righteous actions, it opens to us the blessings of heaven. The man of faith is in control of his life and knows how to get answers to his prayers.

We have been referred to as a believing people. Certainly, faith is the foundation stone of the gospel and the quality that is most important to us as individuals.

Joseph Smith taught: "Faith is the assurance which men have of the existence of things which they have not seen, and the principle of action in all intelligent beings. . . . [It) is the first great governing principle." (*Lectures on Faith,* comp. N. B. Lundwall, Salt Lake City: Bookcraft, n.d., pp. 7, 10.)

Jacob taught that the Lord commands all men to have "perfect faith in the Holy One of Israel, or they cannot be saved in the kingdom of God" (2 Nephi 9:23). As a principle of power and action and as the key to our salvation, our individual faith, then, becomes of absolute importance.

Paul admonished us, "Be thou an example of the believers, in word, in conversation, in charity, in spirit, in faith, in purity" (1 Timothy 4:12). "If ye can no more than desire to believe," said Alma, "let this desire work in you, even until ye believe in a manner that ye can give place for a portion of my words" (Alma 32:27). And Moroni wrote, "Dispute not because ye see

---

Address given at general conference April 1981.

not, for ye receive no witness until after the trial of your faith''
(Ether 12:6).

There are many steps a person can take to develop the gift
and power of faith. I would like to suggest six of these steps.

First: Faith is the ability to recognize the Lord as all-powerful
and as the giver of all blessings. As King Benjamin put it,
''Believe in God; believe that he is, and that he created all
things, both in heaven and in earth; believe that he has all
wisdom, and all power, both in heaven and in earth; believe that
man doth not comprehend all the things which the Lord can
comprehend'' (Mosiah 4:9).

Sometimes we pray about one thing and worry about something else. In doing so we seem to limit the ability of the Lord to
help us in every aspect of our lives.

Elder John A. Widtsoe recorded the following: ''For many
years, under a federal grant with my staff of workers we had
gathered thousands of data in the field of soil moisture; but I
could not extract any general law running through them. I gave
up at last. My wife and I went to the temple that day to forget the
failure. In the third endowment room, out of the unseen, came
the solution, which has long since gone into print.'' (*In a Sunlit
Land: The Autobiography of John A. Widtsoe* [Salt Lake City:
Deseret News Press, 1952], p. 177.)

Faith, then, is the realization that the Lord can help us with
all things.

Second: Faith is the ability to do what we are prompted to
do, and when we are prompted to do it.

A few years ago, while presiding over the Sydney Australia
Mission, I was earnestly seeking a blessing from the Lord. The
mission had done well but was pausing on a plateau, and we
needed to move ahead once again.

On one particular day I was fasting and praying that the Lord
would lead us to a new level of achievement. In the midst of my
prayers came the clear impression to seek out my son, to whom I
am quite close, and give him a blessing. I followed the prompt-
ing and found my oldest son in another part of the house,
attending to his high school studies.

I said, ''How are things going?''

He answered, in typical teenage fashion, ''Why?''

Not knowing what else to say, I asked, "Do you want a blessing?"

He looked at me in stunned silence for a few seconds and then said, "Yes."

The inspiration from that blessing proved to be of great importance to both my son and me. It will be an experience that neither of us will forget. Yet, this would have been lost had I stopped to question why the Lord was turning me to my first responsibility, my family, when I was seeking a blessing for the mission.

Third: Faith is the ability to live the laws of God that control the blessings we need. While we should not keep the commandments just to receive the blessings, it is nevertheless important for us to understand that the blessings are there, predicated upon obedience to specific laws.

Elder Harold B. Lee relates the experience of praying earnestly for a material blessing that he needed badly. One day while he was praying for this blessing, he remembered that he had recently received some income that he had not yet tithed. He said it was as if the accusing voice of the Lord was saying, "You want a blessing from me, but you have not been obedient to the laws upon which such blessings are based." He said that he went and paid the tithing on that income, and then he again sought the particular blessing of the Lord. ("Faith," address delivered at Brigham Young University, June 28, 1955.)

Fourth: Faith is the ability to act "as if."

In his teachings Paul said, "By faith Noah, being warned of God of things not seen . . . prepared an ark to the saving of his house" (Hebrews 11:7). President Spencer W. Kimball gives us this insight concerning Noah and the ark: "As yet there was no evidence of rain or flood. . . . His warnings were considered irrational. . . . How foolish to build an ark on dry ground with the sun shining and life moving forward as usual! But time ran out. . . . The floods came. The disobedient and rebellious were drowned. The miracle of the ark followed the faith manifested in its building." (Spencer W. Kimball, *Faith Precedes the Miracle* [Salt Lake City: Deseret Book Company, 1972], pp. 5–6.)

Many years ago, during the dark days of World War II, the president of the Australian Mission was invited to a faithful widow's house for Sunday dinner. Rationing had taken its toll, and many of the good foods had long since disappeared from the shelves of the local stores.

When the president arrived, he was shocked to find a table filled with the foods that were in short supply.

"I can't eat this food," he said, almost embarrassed that he was taking it out of the mouth of a widow.

"I'm afraid you'll have to," she said. "You see, I listened to the Brethren years ago and put in my year's supply, and this is the only kind of food I have in my pantry."

She had shown the faith to act "as if" by storing food, and her faith produced a miracle in the time of need.

I wonder how many Saints will be able to withstand the disaster of their own personal floods by showing faith in the advice of modern prophets and building an "ark" of family preparedness.

Fifth: Faith is the ability to be charitable and to believe in people.

The Savior of the world is the foremost example of this love. After having been rejected and despised, He asked His Father to forgive those who crucified Him because "they know not what they do" (see Luke 23:34).

Joseph Smith is another example. After living a life filled with trials and betrayals, he said, as he was going to Carthage, "I go like a lamb to the slaughter, yet I have a conscience void of offense toward all men."

I recognized this quality in my own father. On one occasion a person appeared at his door and asked for money. My father said, "I have an old barn that needs painting. If you want to paint it, I'll pay you for it." They went out to look at the barn, and the man was sent to England's paint store to pick up the paint he needed.

The barn was painted, and the man was paid and left town. Shortly after, Mr. England called my father and said that the man had picked up far more paint than was needed to paint the barn. In short, my father had been taken.

My father then took the opportunity to teach his sons a valuable lesson. "Had I known what he did, I would have stopped him," he said. "But we have our painted barn, and the painter, whatever his problems, will always know that there was someone willing to believe in him."

Faith cannot be nourished in a heart that has been made hard by continued cynicism, skepticism, and lack of forgiveness. A person who cannot see the good in people not only destroys his own faith but becomes a basically unhappy person.

Sixth: Faith is the ability to allow ourselves to be guided by the priesthood.

Paul taught us this important truth: "And he [the Lord] gave some, apostles; and some, prophets; and some, evangelists; and some, pastors and teachers." Then he explained why these priesthood leaders were given to the Saints: "Till we all come in the unity of the faith, and of the knowledge of the Son of God, unto a perfect man, unto the measure of the stature of the fulness of Christ" (Ephesians 4:11, 13).

All leaders who have been called by revelation under the hands of the priesthood have been given to us so that we can come to a unity of the faith, that we might know the Savior and have His image in our countenance and become like Him, "that every man might speak in the name of God the Lord, even the Savior of the world" (D&C 1:20).

Years ago, President Joseph Fielding Smith, then a member of the Quorum of the Twelve, attended a stake conference where a relatively new stake president had been called. One man repeatedly came up to President Smith and asked for counsel concerning a personal matter. Finally, President Smith said he would see the man, provided the new stake president could be there. As the man unfolded his situation, the stake president was prompted to know what the person needed to do. Yet President Smith listened to the brother and surprised everyone by saying, "I have no counsel for you." The man promptly left.

After he had gone, President Smith turned to the stake president and said, "I knew how to counsel that man, but I was also prompted to know that he would go against my counsel, so rather than condemn him for going against the counsel of the priesthood, I told him nothing."

From this we learn that it is not enough to merely seek the

direction of those whom God has called to lead us. We must come with a willingness to follow the counsel of inspired leaders in order to develop our faith.

Latter-day Saints need to believe. They need to take every opportunity to develop faith, both in their own lives and in the lives of others.

Faith is a part of our heritage. Those who embrace the gospel of Jesus Christ are the blood of Israel, and characteristic of the house of Israel is the ability to believe. Indeed, some have referred to it as "believing blood."

Let us take advantage of every opportunity to keep our faith alive. By our speech, in our actions, through the commandments we live, and in the way we treat all people, let us build, cultivate, and share this great principle of power in our lives.

Unity in the Faith

To be united is to be at peace with ourselves and with our fellowmen. There is no greater evidence of the true power of the gospel of Jesus Christ in any age than the way it binds the hearts of people together. While the world is seeking to go its own way, the gospel is uniting the hearts of men and women everywhere into a bond of love and brotherhood. Where you find the gospel of Jesus Christ and those imbued by the spirit of the Holy Ghost, you will always find unity.

In this 150th anniversary year of the Church, I would like to center my remarks today on unity in the Church, which comes as the result of keeping the commandments and is attended by the converting and healing power of the Spirit.

In defining conversion as it is used in the scriptures, President Marion G. Romney said:

> It would appear that membership in the Church and conversion are not necessarily synonymous. Being converted . . . and having a testimony are not necessarily the same thing either. A testimony comes when the Holy Ghost gives the earnest seeker a witness of the truth. A moving testimony vitalizes faith; that is, it induces repentance and obedience to the commandments. Conversion, on the other hand, is the fruit of, or the reward for repentance and obedience. . . .
>
> Conversion is effected by divine forgiveness, which remits sins. The sequence is something like this. An honest seeker hears the message. He asks the Lord in prayer if it is true. The Holy Spirit gives him a witness. This is a testimony. If one's testimony is

Devotional address given at Brigham Young University April 1980.

strong enough, he repents and obeys the commandments. By such obedience he receives divine forgiveness which remits sin. Thus he is converted to a newness of life. His spirit is healed. . . .

Somebody recently asked how one could know when he is converted. The answer is simple. He may be assured of it when by the power of the Holy Spirit his soul is healed. When this occurs, he will recognize it by the way he feels, for he will feel as the people of Benjamin felt when they received a remission of sins. The record says, ''. . . The Spirit of the Lord came upon them, and they were filled with joy, having received a remission of their sins, and having peace of conscience. . . .'' (Mosiah 4:3.) (*Improvement Era,* December 1963, p. 1066.)

This definition of conversion brings us to the realization that to be converted is not necessarily the same as receiving a testimony. A person can have a testimony and not be converted. A person can be baptized and not converted. Conversion comes through obedience to the laws of the gospel, which brings a remission of sins and the healing influence of the Spirit.

In missionary work we see this process over and over again—the proper teaching of the gospel; the prayer of faith that brings a glimpse of the truthfulness of the gospel—in other words, a testimony; the desire to repent and become obedient to the commandments, which leads to baptism; and finally, the conferring of the gift of the Holy Ghost, which truly brings a healing spirit to the newly baptized person. He is walking in a newness of life. He feels different. Quite often he looks different. The words *peace* and *joy* can help to describe his frame of mind. This is a change for the better, and everyone is aware of it.

According to those who study the art of communications, it is almost impossible to achieve what is called permanent attitude change. In other words, it is very difficult to change a person's attitudes and expect that change to last.

To me, one of the miracles of the gospel is that men, women, and children from all walks of life, from all ethnic backgrounds, can come to a ''unity of the faith,'' as Paul calls it. (See Ephesians 4:13.) What a remarkable gift is this gift of the Holy Ghost, that it can touch the heart of one who has been baptized and is a worthy seeker! Without robbing that person of his free agency, it can bring him to a unity with the Church, with its leaders, with fellow members, and with good men and women everywhere.

Unity is probably the greatest evidence of conversion. This oneness has been a fundamental characteristic of the gospel of Jesus Christ in all ages. In Romans we read: "So we, being many, are one body in Christ, . . . of the same mind one toward another" (Romans 12:5, 16).

During the persecutions of Missouri and Illinois, the early Saints of this dispensation stood together. When they were united in this spirit and bond of unity, they were blessed and protected. When they began to draw away from this spirit, troubles arose. "[You] are not united according to the union required by the law of the celestial kingdom" (D&C 105:4), the Lord told His suffering Saints in 1834. When individual dissenters began to pull away from the Church, they seemed to follow a pattern. First came the violation of one or more of the basic commandments, usually related to pride. Next was the gradual withdrawal of the Spirit that is always associated with such actions. Then came feelings of disharmony and disunity, eventually followed by outright criticism. It was not the criticism of trying to draw attention to something that may need corrections: such things can be done within the framework of the gospel. Rather it was a criticism that could not be satisfied; criticism that knew no bounds; criticism that grew by feeding upon itself. Says Peter of such a person, "He . . . is blind, and cannot see afar off, and hath forgotten that he was purged from his old sins" (2 Peter 1:9).

A person who yields to the critical spirit has given up the healing influence of the Holy Spirit. He no longer feels the bond of brotherhood and unity that is a gift of the Spirit and the endowment of the Saints of God in all ages.

Just prior to His betrayal and arrest, the Savior urged His disciples to love one another and be united. He also promised them that the Comforter (whom He identified as the Holy Ghost) would come. He then offered this great intercessory prayer, which spoke of unity and oneness as one of the gifts of the Spirit: "Holy Father, keep through thine own name those whom thou hast given me, that they may be one, as we are. . . . Neither pray I for these alone, but for them also which shall believe on

me through their word; That they all may be one." (John 17:11,
20–21.)

Not only does this scripture clearly point out that unity and
oneness must be a characteristic of those in the Lord's church,
but it also shows that the Father and Son are two separate
beings, and that the oneness they enjoy is what they desire for
all the Saints.

That the sanctifying spirit of the Holy Ghost would create
this unity among the faithful Saints was understood. In his
epistle to the Hebrews, Paul makes this clear when he says,
"For both he that sanctifieth and they who are sanctified are all
of one: for which cause he is not ashamed to call them brethren"
(Hebrews 2:11). Sanctification, then, comes from the Savior
through the Holy Ghost.

Following the day of Pentecost, when three thousand were
baptized and received the gift of the Holy Ghost, the record
says: "And they continued stedfastly in the apostles' doctrine
and fellowship. . . . And all that believed were together." (Acts
2:42, 44.)

We read of the city of Enoch prior to its being taken up into
heaven: "And the Lord called his people Zion, because they
were of one heart and one mind, and dwelt in righteousness;
and there was no poor among them" (Moses 7:18).

In Book of Mormon times, after the Savior had appeared to
the people with the fulness of the gospel and as they were living
in peace and in the light of the Spirit, "there were no robbers,
nor murderers, neither were there Lamanites, nor any manner
of -ites; but they were in one, the children of Christ, and heirs to
the kingdom of God" (4 Nephi 1:17).

And what does the Lord say to this generation? "I am Jesus
Christ, the Son of God, who was crucified for the sins of the
world, even as many as will believe on my name, that they may
become the sons of God, even one in me as I am one in the
Father" (D&C 35:2).

Can you catch the spirit of these inspired words? In all dis-
pensations (and this generation is no different), the Lord would
have us embrace the spirit of oneness and peace and unity that
has always been a part of the kingdom of God. It is a unity that
characterizes the relationship between the Father and Son, and

is always a hallmark of the gospel of Jesus Christ. We are a body of Saints following the same leaders, living the same doctrines, opposing the same evils, upholding the same virtues, and moving in the same direction. Each member is guided by the light within him or her, which, coming from the Holy Ghost, will create a perfect bond of unity and determination among the Saints.

One who cultivates the gift of the Spirit comes to the unalterable realization that the Lord is governing His own church through the continuous spirit of revelation, and that our leaders are being inspired by the same Spirit that we are endeavoring to follow. "Whether by mine own voice or by the voice of my servants, it is the same" (D&C 1:38) says the scripture. Such unity is born of the Spirit and is a natural thing for a Church member. Listen to the words of Elder Heber J. Grant on this subject:

> You will always be blessed and benefited by following the advice and counsel of those whom God has chosen to preside over the Church. By honoring the man God has chosen, God will honor and bless you. And as you individually do your duty, you will grow and increase in the light and inspiration of the Spirit of God. As we grow and increase individually, so will the Church grow and increase. (October 1903 Conference Report, p. 10.)

Those who watch us cannot understand this concept, especially in this day and age when the world has put great emphasis on each person's following his own desires and interests. Some may say, "You claim that you believe in individual freedom, yet the great body of the Church follows its leaders, stands for the same principles, upholds the same values." To the world it appears to be blind faith, but quite the opposite is true. It is a oneness born of the Spirit. It is a unity inspired by the spirit of testimony that lies within the hearts of all who have been converted.

President David O. McKay said:

> This testimony has been revealed to every sincere man and woman who has conformed to the principles of the gospel of Jesus Christ, obeyed the ordinances and become entitled to and has received . . . the Holy Ghost, to guide him. Every individual stands independent in his sphere in that testimony, just as [the thousands

of lights do that light up a city] at night, each one of which stands and shines in its own sphere, yet the light in it is produced by the same power, the same energy, from which all the other lights receive their energy. So each individual in the Church stands independently in the knowledge that God lives, that the Savior is the Redeemer of the world, and that the gospel of Jesus Christ has been restored through the Prophet Joseph Smith. (October 1912 Conference Report, pp. 120–126; as printed in *Gospel Ideals: Selections from the Discourses of David O. McKay* [Salt Lake City: *Improvement Era,* 1953].)

No discussion of oneness and unity in the Church would be complete without mention of the united order. This order is a part of the law of consecration. Righteous members of the Church in all ages have consecrated their time, talents, and means to the building up of the Lord's kingdom.

The united order, we are told, rests on three basic principles:

First, the earth is the Lord's. Men are only stewards of their possessions. All that man has should be used therefore in accordance with the Lord's expressed will.

Second, all men are children of God—of a divine family. Therefore, the Lord requires that they must help one another as needs arise, provided that he who will not work shall have no claim upon his brother.

Third, every man must be respected as a free agent. He may enter the order at his pleasure. Once in the order, he must be allowed to use, fully and as he pleases, any properties placed in his hands. He may leave the order at his pleasure. (John A. Widtsoe, *Joseph Smith* [Salt Lake City: Deseret News Press, 1951], p. 192.)

These principles of the united order reflect, again, the divine standards of unity among the Saints, while at the same time preserving free agency. We are told that the time will come when, as Saints, we will be required to live the law of consecration more perfectly; this, of course, will include the united order.

I have endeavored to point out, thus far, the following things:

1. That a person cannot receive a fulness of the gospel unless he is converted.

2. That conversion may not be the same as receiving a testimony or even being baptized.

3. That conversion, as Elder Romney has defined it from the scriptures, is having our sins remitted and being healed by the Spirit. The words *peace* and *joy* are used in this context.

4. That one of the clearest manifestations of the true gospel of Jesus Christ in all ages is the oneness and unity of its righteous members—unity between the individual and the Savior; unity among its leaders; unity and loyalty among the entire membership.

5. That the Spirit naturally creates this unity and oneness, especially among those who have been converted. Such unity and oneness among the members also brings the Spirit into their lives.

6. That the world cannot always understand this unity, because it cannot understand the workings of the Spirit as it binds the Church together.

Why do I choose this particular topic? Because in every age there are voices challenging that unity—voices from within and voices from without. Perhaps they challenge your unity with the Savior. Perhaps they challenge your unity with your Church leaders. Perhaps they challenge your unity with the Church itself.

My friends, if you are to stand unitedly with the Church, then seek the kinds of experiences that will put you on a firm footing so that outside voices do not detract.

A number of years ago, when my family and I were living in Boston, I had just finished a particularly bad week. You know what a bad week is, don't you? It's seven straight bad days. By the end of the week I was feeling down and a bit sorry for myself. Finally, one night after my family had gone to bed, I determined to stay up longer and really go before the Lord in a more determined way than when I said my regular night and morning prayers.

As I knelt in the downstairs study of that darkened house, my circumstances made it easy to approach the Lord in the depths of humility, and I poured out my heart. As I prayed, I felt the need for a confirmation that He was there and that He cared. From past experiences I knew these things, but there are times when one needs the strength of reconfirmation. As I prayed and made this specific request, I had a most remarkable experience. I had had spiritual experiences before, but this, to me, was more. There was an outpouring of the Spirit, so real that I could feel it. It filled my whole soul, and was not just a single experience, but came again and again in the space of just a minute or two.

I came from that room that night with a reconfirmed and absolute knowledge, born of the Spirit, that not only did the Savior live but also that He knew me and cared for me with a love that was truly divine.

The influence of that experience lingered with me for days and caused me to feel genuine concern and love for my fellow-man. While previously I would pass unfamiliar people on the street with little or no thought, I now felt a concern for and interest in them. My family, if it were possible, were more dear to me. I felt a bond with the Saints everywhere and wanted to serve my fellowman.

I can't remember the trials I was facing at that particular time. They passed, as trials usually do. But I will always remember the experience of that evening when the Spirit healed me. It reconfirmed to me that if our hearts are right, we can go before the Lord, and, in one degree or another and in one way or another, He will send the healing influence of the Spirit. And the Spirit not only heals, but it also unites. This need not be a singular experience, but can happen often.

Elder Heber C. Kimball, speaking of those who would have liked to live at the time of the Prophet Joseph Smith, said:

> You imagine that you would have stood by him when persecution raged and he was assailed by foes within and without. You would have defended him and been true to him in the midst of every trial. You think you would have been delighted to have shown your integrity in the days of mobs and traitors.
>
> Let me say to you, that many of you will see the time when you will have all the trouble, trial, and persecution that you can stand, and plenty of opportunities to show that you are true to God and his work. This Church has before it many close places through which it will have to pass before the work of God is crowned with victory. To meet the difficulties that are coming, it will be necessary for you to have a knowledge of the truth of this work for yourselves.

If you have not got the testimony, live right and call upon the Lord and cease not till you obtain it. . . . The time will come when no man nor woman will be able to endure on borrowed light. Each will have to be guided by the light within himself. (Orson F. Whitney, *Life of Heber C. Kimball* [Salt Lake City: Bookcraft, 1967], pp. 449–50.)

What, then, can a person do to invite the healing and uniting influence of the Spirit into his or her life?

The scriptures and writings of the Brethren are filled with helps and aids. Let me list just a few that have been helpful to me:

1. Keep the commandments as a means of receiving the Spirit. President Joseph Fielding Smith said, "We have the right to the guidance of the Holy Ghost, but we cannot have that guidance, if we willfully refuse to consider the revelations that have been given to help us to understand and to guide us in the light and the truth of the everlasting gospel" (Joseph Fielding Smith, *Doctrines of Salvation,* comp. Bruce R. McConkie, 3 vols. [Salt Lake City: Bookcraft, 1954–56], 1:43).

2. Learn to identify the impressions of the Spirit. The Lord has told us, "I will tell you in your mind and in your heart, by the Holy Ghost" (D&C 8:2), and "you shall feel that it is right" (D&C 9:8). He also says that we must "study it out" in our minds (see D&C 9:8).

These impressions of truth are usually associated with peace, warmth, and assurance. You will find that such impressions will be in harmony with the scriptures, with the Church, and usually with good common sense. If you are unsure about your promptings, discuss the matter with your priesthood leaders. I have come to realize that the Lord prompts us far more than we sometimes think. For many, the challenge is not in receiving promptings by the Spirit, but in following them.

3. Pray earnestly. President Joseph F. Smith said these inspired words:

It is not such a difficult thing to learn how to pray. It is not the words we use particularly that constitute prayer. . . . True, faithful, earnest prayer consists more in the feeling that arises from the heart and from the inward desire of our spirits to supplicate the Lord in humility and in faith, that we may receive his blessings. It

matters not how simple the words may be, if our desires are
genuine and we come before the Lord with a broken heart and contrite spirit to ask him for that which we need. (Joseph F. Smith,
Gospel Doctrine [Salt Lake City: Deseret Book Company, 1966],
p. 219.)

4. Keep the Sabbath day holy. The consolidated schedule
will help us catch the spirit of this day. While I was growing up
my family kept the Sabbath day. We took part in no sports or
everyday activities. There is a spirit about this day that will
truly heal the soul, because it is centered on partaking the sacrament, where we can shed harmful thoughts and actions and
receive an increase of the Spirit. The Sabbath can heal us for the
week ahead. Don't just keep the Sabbath, but catch the spirit of
the Sabbath.

5. Pay an honest tithing. This law brings both spiritual and
temporal blessings.

6. Be careful of too much scheduling and long-range
planning, because it can shut out inspiration. Sometimes our
schedule is so tight that the Lord can't get through. Other times
it is so loose that when He does get through there is no discipline
to carry out what needs to be done. A balance is needed.

7. Be an example of the believer. Don't damage your faith
and the faith of others by constantly taking the role of the
"devil's advocate." There are other ways to clarify issues and
bring up questions. Become known as a person who sheds light
on a matter and not as a professional dissenter.

8. Get a basic testimony. A person who has received assur-
ances from the Spirit that God lives, that Jesus is the Christ, that
Joseph Smith was a prophet, and that the Church President is a
prophet today, will have faith sufficient to meet everyday issues
until such time as the Lord provides all the "hows" and
"whys." "For ye receive no witness," wrote Moroni, "until
after the trial of your faith" (Ether 12:6).

9. Don't compartmentalize. Seek the Spirit and take the
principles of the gospel into every avenue of your life. The
gospel embraces all truth; allow it to do so.

10. Get an early witness of the divine calling of each of your
leaders. Do not decide in advance who you are and are not going

to follow, or what leader you like or don't like. Seek an early witness of that person's calling.

11. Develop charity. A person who is basically forgiving has an easier time cultivating the Spirit than one who finds it hard to forgive.

12. Study the scriptures daily, especially the Book of Mormon. This need only be a few minutes, but you will feel the difference.

May the Lord bless us all that we might have His healing Spirit to be with us and that by the power and peace of that Spirit we might be one in purpose, one in unity, one in sustaining each other. May we "keep the unity of the Spirit in the bond of peace" (Ephesians 4:3).

If there are any at this time who, for one reason or another, have found themselves running contrary to that unity and peace, with all the energy of my soul I invite you back—back to the Lord's church; back to the peace of the gospel; back to the healing influence of the Spirit; back to those who will stand with you and will care for you; back to unity in the faith.

To those who have not yet experienced this, we invite you to come and be one with us. Receive the commandments. Join with the Saints and let the Spirit heal you.

The Spirit Giveth Life

In order to know God and to prepare ourselves to live in the kingdom where He is, we must somehow change our nature from the "natural man" to a new being in the image of the Savior. This is the role of the Holy Spirit, and if we keep the covenants of the gospel of Jesus Christ, it will bring a spirit that will gradually change our nature and prepare us for eternal life.

The most unique feature of The Church of Jesus Christ of Latter-day Saints is that it is governed by the Savior, through the promptings and direction of the Spirit.

Those called to serve will prayerfully seek the inspiration of the Spirit to supplement and even go beyond their own natural abilities. Whenever the Church is upon the earth, there is always this reference to the Spirit as a guide. This is true, no matter what the background of the leaders might be.

Two classic examples of this are Paul, the great New Testament prophet, and Brigham Young, the second President of the Church. Paul was a Pharisee and a pupil of Gamaliel. In addition to this, he was a member of the Sanhedrin. If anyone could approach his work with the credentials of an intellectual and a scholar, he could. Yet after his conversion, he was very careful to draw a distinction between these two approaches. In his letter to the Corinthians, he said: "Now we have received, not the spirit of the world, but the spirit which is of God; that we might know the things that are freely given to us of God. Which things also we speak, not in the words which man's wisdom

Address given at general conference April 1979.

teacheth, but which the Holy Ghost teacheth; comparing spiritual things with spiritual." (1 Corinthians 2:12–14; see also verse 11.)

Brigham Young was practical, level-headed, and down-to-earth. A glazier by trade, he became the second President of the Church after the death of the Prophet Joseph Smith. He led the Saints into a trackless waste and kept them from perishing until they forged a new life by making the desert blossom as the rose (see Isaiah 35:1). He recognized the practical and sensible aspects of religious life and service to God; yet from this down-to-earth, practical prophet come these words: "The eye, the ear, the hand, all the senses may be deceived, but the Spirit of God cannot be deceived; and when inspired with that Spirit, the whole man is filled with knowledge, he can see with a spiritual eye, and he knows that which is beyond the power of man to controvert" (*Journal of Discourses,* 16:46).

We learn from these two great prophets that there is need to go beyond the word and find the power and strength that can come from the Spirit.

When we speak of the Spirit, we refer to the gift of the Holy Ghost. While the light of Christ enlightens all who come into the world, the spirit of the Holy Ghost is something more. The Holy Ghost is the third member of the Godhead; a personage of spirit, he speaks not for himself, but testifies to all that Jesus is the Christ, the Son of God, and conveys to man the mind and will of the Lord (see John 16:13–15). He has a sanctifying and cleansing influence upon the souls of men and is the source of spiritual gifts. Just as Paul tells us that there is one Lord, one faith, and one baptism (see Ephesians 4:5), so this gift of the Holy Ghost can only come in one way. Only the right authority is acceptable for baptism and conferring the gift of the Holy Ghost, and this was made clear when Paul traveled to Ephesus and rebaptized some who had not been baptized with the right authority, and then conferred upon them the Holy Ghost (see Acts 19).

While the Spirit of the Holy Ghost will witness to a person that this is the gospel of Jesus Christ, the gift of the Holy Ghost comes only after a person has been baptized into the Church. It can be identified with feelings of peace and assurance to the prayerful and honest seeker for truth, and thus the scripture: "Yea, behold, I will tell you in your mind and in your heart, by the Holy Ghost, which shall come upon you and which shall dwell in your heart" (D&C 8:2). "Therefore, you shall feel that it is right" (D&C 9:8).

Some think that our ultimate judgment and reward will be based on how many laws and commandments we keep and how many we do not keep. While in a sense this is true, it misses the broader and spiritual purpose for keeping the commandments. When I was younger, I lived to play basketball. It was on my mind constantly. I spent countless hours practicing. Gradually I began to go through the moves automatically, without thinking about them. Physically and mentally I had become conditioned to do certain things by instinct. I had practiced them until they became natural to me.

In like manner, we keep the commandments and teachings of the gospel in order to condition us spiritually. It is not a matter of how many laws we keep and how many we do not keep. We keep the commandments because they are the laws that govern the Spirit. The Spirit in turn will sanctify us, condition us spiritually, and eventually prepare us to live in the kingdom where God is. Hence the scripture: "They who are not sanctified through the law which I have given unto you, even the law of Christ, must inherit another kingdom" (D&C 88:21). The laws that govern the Spirit are nothing more or less than the laws that govern the Church. In addition, there is also an outpouring of the Spirit for those loyal to and willing to uphold the prophet and others who have been called to preside.

That the Spirit can and should have power in our lives and that we can have definite and measurable experiences associated with the Spirit is quite clear. One need only refer to the great variety of gifts of the Spirit promised to all who live the laws and commandments of Christ.

We should seek the Spirit through the prayer of faith and through keeping the commandments, including partaking of the sacrament worthily, so that we might "have his Spirit to be with [us]" (D&C 20:79).

The sons of Mosiah, for instance, were fasting and praying in preparation for their mission to the Lamanites; they wanted a portion of the Spirit of the Lord to go with them and abide with them. The answer is recorded in this verse: "And it came to pass that the Lord did visit them with his Spirit, and said unto them: Be comforted. And they were comforted." (Alma 17:10.) Would you not be comforted if the Lord, by His Spirit, gave you the same experience?

The prophet Alma says: "And now behold, I ask of you, my brethren of the church, have ye spiritually been born of God? Have ye received his image in your countenances? Have ye experienced this mighty change in your hearts?" (Alma 5:14.)

Alma was making sure that the members of the Church had not just received the gift of the Holy Ghost, but also had truly received the sanctifying and cleansing power of that great Spirit. He said the way you can tell is when you become refreshed spiritually, as if you had been born anew. He said that the feelings and attitudes of your heart will be truly changed for the good. That your very appearance will begin to take upon itself the image of God.

What a great and powerful friend is this gift of the Holy Ghost! Certainly all who will turn to the Savior and abide by His laws will be healed by this Spirit (see 3 Nephi 9:13). They will have the mind of Christ (see 1 Corinthians 2:16), they will be "partakers of the divine nature" (see 2 Peter 1:4), they will begin to have the image of Christ in their countenances (see Alma 5:14). Truly the gospel comes, as Paul said, not only in word, "but also in power," the sanctifying, cleansing, soul-enlarging power of the Holy Spirit (1 Thessalonians 1:5).

After the death of the Prophet Joseph Smith, Brigham Young had a dream in which Joseph Smith appeared to him with the following advice: "Tell the brethren to keep their hearts open to conviction, so that when the Holy Ghost comes to them, their hearts will be ready to receive it. They can tell the Spirit of the Lord from all other spirits; it will whisper peace and joy to their souls; it will take malice, hatred, strife and all evil from their hearts; and their whole desire will be to do good, bring forth righteousness and build up the kingdom of God. Tell the brethren if they will follow the spirit of the Lord they will go right. Be sure to tell the people to keep the Spirit,'' he said. (*Manuscript History of Brigham Young 1846–1847*, pub. by Elden J. Watson [Salt Lake City, 1971], pp. 529–30.)

And these final words from the Doctrine and Covenants: "Therefore, sanctify yourselves that your minds become single to God, and the days will come that you shall see him; for he will unveil his face unto you, and it shall be in his own time, and in his own way, and according to his own will" (D&C 88:68).

And thus we have the end result of the workings of the Spirit, to bring us face to face with Jesus Christ, our Savior and Redeemer.

Loyalty to the prophets and prayerful obedience to the word of God will bring the power of the Spirit. The enlarging influence of the Spirit will sanctify us, will condition us spiritually, and prepare us to see him face to face and converse as one speaketh to another, and to live in his kingdom, even the celestial kingdom.

> The witness of the Holy Ghost
> As borne by those who know,
> Has lifted me again to thee,
> O Father of my soul.
>
> While listening to them testify,
> The Spirit fills my heart,
> Dispels the gloom, confirms the right,
> Pure truth it does impart.
>
> I know that thou art in thy heav'n,
> I know the Savior reigns;
> I know a prophet speaks to us
> For our eternal gain.
>
> The Holy Spirit moves all doubt,
> It lights the heart of man.
> It says to all, "Return to me,
> Come, follow my great plan."
>
> My eyes are wet, my heart is full,
> The Spirit speaks today.
> Oh Lord, wilt thou my life renew
> And in my bosom stay.

As testimony fills my heart,
It dulls the pain of days;
For one brief moment heaven's view
Is fixed before my gaze.

May the Lord help us to reach beyond the words of life and to capture this great spirit, I pray. In the name of Jesus Christ, amen.

This Is His Church

The words and teachings of the gospel of Jesus Christ are designed for one basic purpose—to turn people to the Lord. Each seeker after the truth needs to apply the words of salvation and receive his own witness that Jesus is the Christ and that this work is true. This becomes his personal testimony. In the final analysis, although we can help one another, it is left up to each individual to gain his own witness and receive the peace that comes from allowing the power of heaven to confirm the truth to us.

A young friend of ours approached my wife and me recently, anxious to share an experience which, although seemingly insignificant, had changed her life.

She had been given an assignment to speak at a sacrament meeting the previous Sunday. As she began to gather notes in preparation for her talk, she just didn't feel right about what she was planning to say. Finally, she put everything aside and went to her room, where she knelt and prayed for inspiration and guidance. Soon she was touched deeply by the Spirit.

As she went back to her preparation, she was inspired by a clarity of thought she had not experienced before. Because of this, she delivered what others described as an exceptionally good and inspirational sacrament meeting talk.

In telling this experience she said, "You know, this may sound strange to you, but this has made me a different person. I have been a member of the Church all my life, but it wasn't until

---

Address given at general conference October 1968.

I knelt to pray about this talk that I discovered the Lord really does watch over me and He honestly cares.''

This discovery caused me to think of the words of Enos in the Book of Mormon, when he said:

> Behold, it came to pass that I, Enos, knowing my father that he was a just man—for he taught me in his language, and also in the nurture and admonition of the Lord—and blessed be the name of my God for it—
>
> And I will tell you of the wrestle which I had before God, before I received a remission of my sins.
>
> Behold, I went to hunt beasts in the forests; and the words which I had often heard my father speak concerning eternal life, and the joy of the saints, sunk deep into my heart.
>
> And my soul hungered; and I kneeled down before my Maker, and I cried unto him in mighty prayer and supplication. (Enos 1:1–4.)

Enos had been raised by good parents. According to his own words, he had been taught by his parents ''in the nurture and admonition of the Lord.'' Yet there was a sort of gap between what his parents knew and what he knew.

One day Enos went to hunt beasts in the forest. The words he had heard his father speak about eternal life and the joy of the Saints sank deep into his heart, and it was then that he had to know for himself. Quite often this is the pattern of young people today. They hear the words of their parents and Church teachers. Sometimes these words are not of personal value until they reach the point of wanting to know for themselves, or until such time as these words are challenged, or there is some other experience that prompts them to action.

Enos wanted to know, and because of the teachings of his parents, he knew how to find out—and he did.

How different from Enos's experience was the recent experience of a college student who had also heard all the familiar words from his teachers and others as he was growing up. But this young man had not discovered if these things were true prior to the time he engaged in a particular course of study, which, he believed, challenged his faith in The Church of Jesus Christ of Latter-day Saints.

He subsequently rejected the words without ever finding out if they were true. And, in a sense, he became inactive in the Church without ever having been *in* the Church—or at least without ever having experienced the spiritual blessings of the Church.

There are those who see this Church from the outside and marvel at its programs and organization. They ask how this is accomplished, expecting that in a few sentences a formula will be given that they can take back and apply to their own organization.

The success and vitality of the Church, however, lie in something that is unseen. It is the power and Spirit that enlightens the person who gains for himself a true knowledge that God and Jesus Christ are actually divine, living beings, and that this is the Church of Jesus Christ revealed from God and is not devised by man.

To know this is to be free from many doubts and frustrations. To know this is to be able to look ahead with confidence, courage, and peace of mind. And to know this is to know that God is actually there and that His love for us is both personal and real.

When the pressures and problems of life become too great, one can always retreat to this testimony for comfort, solace, and renewed strength.

I suppose there are many ways to gain this knowledge, but I know of none more sure than by means of these two promises:

Inasmuch as ye shall keep my commandments . . . ye shall know that it is by me that ye are led. (1 Nephi 17:13.)

Calling on the name of the Lord for the Comforter, which shall teach them all things that are expedient for them—

Praying always that they faint not; and inasmuch as they do this, I will be with them even unto the end. (D&C 75:10–11.)

Chances are, if you are a young member of this Church, that you have heard these words many times before. Perhaps now is the time, if you have not already done so, to do as Enos did and gain your own testimony that the Lord lives and that He directs the affairs of His church.

His promise is that if you live the standards that He has set down, and read the Book of Mormon with faith and prayerful intent, He will manifest these things unto you by the power of the Holy Ghost.

I think of the words of President David O. McKay, who has declared: "He is our Head. This is His church. Without His divine guidance and constant inspiration, we cannot succeed; with His guidance, with His inspiration, we cannot fail."

To this I humbly add my witness that I know that God lives; that Jesus Christ is His Son and the Savior of the world; that a prophet of God restored this church; that a prophet of God stands at the head of this church today; and that this church is led by revelation.

God knows and loves and cares, and He is most anxious that you, young people, draw close to Him so that He can, by the Holy Ghost, arm you with this divine knowledge.

II.
Love
And Unity

_Oh, parents, no matter what the difficulty, may we never
desert our children in some dark and dangerous
thoroughfare of life, no matter what prompted them to get
there. When they reach the point that they need
us—and for some it may be a painfully long time—I pray
that we might not let them down._

Our Precious Families

Although no home is perfect and no parent is free from mistakes, there are certain principles we can stand for and pass on to the next generation of home builders as being important.

Our greatest contribution to our children may be what they see as they look back at what we stood for and wanted most for those we loved.

I would like to use as the key to my remarks a statement that President Spencer W. Kimball made on a previous occasion. He said, "The nation is built upon the foundation of its homes and the home upon its families." The family—mother and father and children—is the oldest of all our institutions and stands at the very foundation of our civilization. There can be nothing more precious or enduring than the family.

It is obvious, however, that the need exists for upgrading the role of parents in the family setting.

A few years ago, I went on a business trip to eastern Canada with a broad range of business and community leaders. After the business of the day, we had dinner together. During the course of the evening, as everyone began to relax and get better acquainted, one of those present, for no apparent reason, began to tell about his son—a boy whom he obviously loved very much. Yet there was conflict in their relationship and even some alienation, and he wasn't sure what to do or if indeed he should do anything.

Address given in general conference October 1974.

That comment prompted similar responses from the others seated around the table. You could tell it was something they were not used to talking about, but each was personally concerned about some aspect of his family life, and this concern was primarily associated with his children.

Although we live in an era of transition and change, I believe parents are as anxious and concerned about their children as they have ever been. If the family is the foundation of society, then perhaps there is need to reaffirm some basic principles.

First, parents need to recognize they have the right to structure the attitudes and conduct of their children. It is not only their right, but their responsibility.

Second, the principle of work—the work ethic, if you please—should be taught by the parents in the family setting. Where else is the dignity of work to be taught if not in the home?

And third, parents have the right to establish the moral and spiritual tone in the family, and to help family members realize the importance of living divine principles as a means of accomplishment and peace of mind.

Let me review each of these principles in greater detail. First, then, is the right of parents to structure the attitudes and conduct of their children. Fundamentally, this is a divine right. God said of Abraham that he "shall surely become a great and mighty nation. . . . For I know him, that he will command his children and his household after him, and they shall keep the way of the Lord, to do justice and judgment." (Genesis 18:18–19.) God could make Abraham head of a numerous posterity because of his faithfulness in teaching his children.

There are some in the world who might say that such parental influence is repressive and robs the child of his or her freedom. Quite the opposite is true. A group of young girls was once overheard talking about the parents of one of their friends. Showing maturity beyond her years, one of the girls said, "Her parents don't love her; they let her do anything she wants." The others agreed.

In a *New York Times Magazine* article, later condensed in *Reader's Digest,* William V. Shannon made the following points: "American children are suffering from widespread parent failure. By their words and actions many fathers and mothers make it clear that they are almost paralyzed by uncertainty. . . . Many parents are in conflict as to what their own values are. Others think they know, but lack the confidence to impose discipline in behalf of their values."

What is lacking, he said, is not more information on child development, but *conviction*. Although heredity plays some role in the development of a child, the greater influence "depends on whether parents care enough about their children to assert and defend the necessary values." Furthermore, both mother and father need to put home responsibilities first. "Rearing our children is by far the most important task that most of us will ever undertake."

He also stated that "parents who do not persevere in rearing their children according to their own convictions are not leaving them 'free' to develop on their own. Instead, they are letting other children and the media, principally television and the movies, do the job." (William V. Shannon, "What Code of Values Can We Teach Our Children?" *Reader's Digest,* May 1972, pp. 187–88.)

The greatest principle to be learned in the family setting is love. If parents will influence and direct and persevere with love, then members of the family will also make that principle a part of all they do. The principle of love can overcome many personal mistakes made in the raising of children. But love should not be confused with lack of conviction.

Second, the principle of work should be taught in the family and home setting.

There is a little farm on the edge of Tooele where my father was born. It was on this farm, when my brother and I were teenagers, that my father decided we needed to learn how to work.

My father was running the newspaper in town and was president of a stake that covered a hundred square miles. He was pretty busy, but he had us working on that farm. We were in the 4-H program, and some of the fathers of the boys in the 4-H program bought some purebred, registered Guernseys, and we each got a cow. I should say my brother got a cow, and since I was his little brother, it was mine by association. I don't know how many of you have had experience with cows, but our cow had heifer after heifer after heifer, and, when you get a heifer, you end up with another cow; and, when you end up with another cow, that's one more cow to milk. It was not very long until we were sort of in the business. We had a number of cows we were milking, and it was quite an experience.

We had some great unsupervised experiences on the farm, my brother and I. I think he was more steady than I was. We had some fruit trees and a lot of hay. We grew some corn; we grew a little wheat. We had a number of things on that farm. We weren't the best farmers in the world. We were doing the best we could, but we were not the best farmers. We were surrounded by other farms, and those farms were being run by people who knew what they were doing. One day one of the neighbors went to my father. He had a whole list of the things that my brother and I were doing wrong. I think I could have added more things to that list than he had. Anyway, he went down the list as he was talking to my father, and my father just sat back and listened. Then he said, "Jim, you don't understand. You see, I'm raising boys, not cows." A few years after my father passed away, Jim shared that experience with me.

In spite of the mistakes, we learned how to work on that little farm; and I guess, although they didn't say it in so many words, we always knew we were more important to Mother and Father than the cows—or, for that matter, anything else.

Certainly in every home, all family members can be given responsibilities that will fall within their ability to accomplish, and at the same time teach them the satisfaction and dignity of work.

The third point is that parents have the right to teach moral and spiritual principles to their children. In that regard, let me quote the following from modern scripture: "And again, inasmuch as parents have children in Zion, or in any of her stakes which are organized, that teach them not to understand the doctrine of repentance, faith in Christ the Son of the living God, and of baptism and the gift of the Holy Ghost by the laying on of the hands, when eight years old, the sin be upon the heads of the parents" (D&C 68:25).

In his first address to the United States Congress, President Gerald Ford stated this universal truth: "If we can make effective . . . use of the moral and ethical wisdom of the centuries in today's complex society, we will prevent more crime and corruption than all the policemen and prosecutors . . . can ever deter." And he added: "This is a job that must begin at home, not in Washington." (*Christian Science Monitor,* August 28, 1974.)

In the article previously mentioned, Mr. Shannon said: "Nothing has invalidated the hard-earned moral wisdom that mankind has accumulated since biblical times. To kill, to steal, to lie, or to covet another person's possessions still leads to varying degrees of misery for the victim and the perpetrator. . . . 'Thou shalt not commit adultery' may sound old-fashioned, but restated in contemporary terms—'Do not smash up another person's family life'—still carries a worthwhile message."

He also pointed out the virtues of self-denial and anticipation. As older teenagers learn the facts about sex, it would do no harm, he stated, to use self-control. "A certain amount of frustration and tension can be endured—and with good effect. Only modern Americans," he wrote, "regard frustration as ranking higher than cholera in the scale of human afflictions."

These are but three of many principles that should be emphasized in the setting of family and home.

The next question is, how do parents get this accomplished? For members of the Church, the point at which this training and communication begins in the family is family home evening. Monday night is set aside for the family, and nothing interferes. The head of the family takes the lead, but other members of the family also prepare and participate. What is said and done depends on the needs of that particular family. The Church has published some guidelines to help parents teach moral and religious principles to the family, and make them apply in everyday life.

May the Lord bless us as parents to realize our right to help develop the lives of our children, to teach the dignity of work, and to establish moral and religious principles in our homes.

This Is My Beloved Son

Since the turn of the century, the role between a father and his children has gradually changed. When America was primarily an agricultural society, a father and his children usually worked side by side in the fields. As society changed, the father went away to work, and the mother, more often than not, shouldered the burden of raising the children.

There is an ongoing need for fathers to understand what their Heavenly Father would expect of them. There is a need for us as fathers to use balance in our lives with an ever-watchful and loving eye on the members of our own families.

From section 68 of the Doctrine and Covenants come these familiar words:

> And again, inasmuch as parents have children in Zion, or in any of her stakes which are organized, that teach them not to understand the doctrine of repentance, faith in Christ the Son of the living God, and of baptism and the gift of the Holy Ghost by the laying on of the hands, when eight years old, the sin be upon the heads of the parents.
>
> For this shall be a law unto the inhabitants of Zion, or in any of her stakes which are organized.
>
> And their children shall be baptized for the remission of their sins when eight years old, and receive the laying on of the hands.
>
> And they shall also teach their children to pray, and to walk uprightly before the Lord. (D&C 68:25–28.)

To help us with these sacred responsibilities, the Lord has given us family home evening. But at the basis of a successful

---

Address given at general conference October 1971.

home evening has to be the proper relationship between the parents and the other members of the family. For instance, I believe there is no finer relationship in all the world than the special one that can exist between a father and his children—a relationship born of love and those deep, abiding feelings that exist initially by instinct and are later nurtured and developed by love and kindness and consideration.

I mention here the relationship of a father to his children not to demean in any way the tremendous role of the mother; but, having never been a mother, I feel that I am not qualified to speak from that point of view. Not only that, but I firmly believe that, generally speaking, the mothers of the Church are in need of a little more help from the fathers of the Church in building those special ties between parents and children.

I am impressed by the fact that the plan of redemption and salvation for all mankind was worked out between a father and his son, even God the Father and His Son Jesus Christ.

I believe that one of the significant parts of the Joseph Smith story was when the angel Moroni told young Joseph to go to his father and relate to him everything that had happened. Even in the restoration of the gospel of Jesus Christ the Lord was careful to recognize the relationship of this young boy to his father, and He made sure that nothing would damage it.

Yes, the association of a father with his children can and should be a very special one.

Certainly the outcome of children's lives cannot always be predicted, and sometimes under the best circumstances something happens that will cause a member of the family to go astray. While these things are sometimes hard to understand, nevertheless, more than one life has been retrieved and altered for the good because of the undying love of a father for his son or daughter—a love that will tend to ease the frustrations that young people experience as they try to find themselves amid a conflict of ideals and standards.

One commentator talked about a typical youth of today in these terms:

> He is told he must be strong, beautiful, brave, and so on—a Boy Scout with jet-set sophistication.
>
> He is swamped with plugs for beer, cigarettes, credit cards, and trips to Hawaii.

To a girl it is suggested that she is a failure unless she looks like a . . . Hollywood queen.

No wonder the poor child feels pain when he measures himself against what he is told is the ideal.

How to ease the minds of the young is one of the hardest things.

It is no good to say it doesn't matter, because it does.

It is not good to say that it only hurts for a little while, like hanging.

But it might help if the youngster could be convinced that, in spite of the mismatch between himself and the false ideals held up before him, he possesses as much human worth as the next one and need not despair.

This conflict of ideals and standards between what a young person is taught to do by the Church and what is expected by the world creates tremendous frustration. Certainly a father is in the best position to begin to bring these things into perspective, to help his son or daughter understand what is important in life, to be there to reassure and to love and to make his children feel important, and to help them to be themselves and to stay close to their standards.

Someone once said that the middle-aged and the old forget how keenly the young are affected, and by what. The young haven't had any experience with this amazing process called youth, and we all need to realize that.

As a father in the Church attempts to be a father to his children, there are occasionally some special conflicts. For example, the Lord said: "And again, verily I say unto you, that every man who is obliged to provide for his own family, let him provide, and he shall in nowise lose his crown; and let him labor in the church" (D&C 75:28). This spells out two basic responsibilities —providing for our families and laboring in the Church. Questions sometimes arise as to a seeming conflict between a father's duty to his family and the many Church responsibilities which might be his.

Certainly all Church leaders who have responsibility for organizing and calling administrative meetings should realize that a well-planned, well-organized meeting, with beginning and ending times determined in advance, will not only make the maximum use of time but will make it easier for the brethren who attend these meetings to receive the support of their wives and children. A well-planned meeting means that the family knows when they can expect the husband or father home. A well-planned meeting cuts down on the number of intermediate meetings that might needlessly take the father away from the home. Certainly well-planned and well-scheduled meetings are as much a blessing to the families of the Church as they are to those fathers who attend the meetings.

On the other hand, the Lord expects us to take care of our families as well as attending to our duties in the Church.

It may not always be true that a heavy load of Church responsibilities is the reason a father does not draw close to his family.

My father was a stake president for twenty years. He was called when I was six and released when I was twenty-six. I can hardly remember a time in my youth when he was not stake president. He had a very large stake, and it took a great deal of his time.

In addition to this he was a newspaper editor, and there were always demanding deadlines and other work that simply could not be put off. I can remember that a seventeen-, eighteen-, or nineteen-hour day was not unusual for him.

While this could have created difficulties with us as children in our relationship with our father, surprisingly it did not. In reflecting on what he did to keep us close to him, even though he had virtually no time to spend with us, I believe it was his ability to build us into his life. Even on the run, he knew what we were doing and was vitally interested and cared. His questions and comments let us know that he was proud of us and interested in us and followed us, although he could not always be with us.

I also remember that no matter how tired he and Mother must have been, they never went to sleep until we were home.

When I was the only one left at home, he would not hold family prayer until I came home, even though he and Mother would be in bed. In situations like that he always called on me to pray—and that had quite an impact on how I conducted myself as a youth, when I knew that I was going to have to end my evening at the bedside of my parents in prayer.

In addition to that, we would have some very profound discussions during those quiet, uninterrupted late-night hours. He was always willing to talk if I wanted to talk, no matter what the hour.

I would have to say that my father was the greatest man I ever knew, although he didn't have a great deal of time to spend with me.

As I look back on it, I realize that although the amount of time we spend is important, probably the most important thing is our ability to build our children into our lives. If we can express sincere interest in them, and let them know that we know what is going on, even if we have to do it on the run sometimes, this seems to be far more important than a parent who has more time but somehow does not convey this interest.

Finally, may I emphasize how preciously short the time is for a father to influence his children. In the United States and Canada, if your child is nine years old he has already spent approximately one-half of the time he is going to spend in your home. By the time a young person is eighteen, he may be off to school or otherwise beginning his own life. By the time he is nineteen, he is on his mission. In some countries around the world, the time is even shorter.

I was with a bishop the other day who told me of how his eight-year-old daughter woke him up in the middle of the night to ask him a question. The next morning the bishop patiently explained to the girl that he was a very busy man and had a lot of work to do and needed his sleep, so he would be most grateful if she didn't wake him up in the middle of the night.

The little girl waited patiently, and finally, in an almost exasperated manner, she said, "Yes, Daddy, but you don't understand. You see, you are the bishop, and I had a problem."

In this sense, may each of us be the bishops of our own home, just as the duly authorized bishop is the father of his ward. I would hope, too, that the bishop of the ward and the home teachers would be especially attentive to those families permanently or temporarily without fathers in their homes.

May we take the time to do what we need and want to do with our children *now*, before it is too late, because the days have a way of escaping into months and then to years.

May we strive to rededicate ourselves and strengthen our relationships with our children, and to lend even greater help and leadership to the lovely mothers of this Church as we work to bring the principles of righteousness, truth, joy, peace, and happiness to the youth of our families.

Can They Count On Us?

The bond that develops when parents never give up on their children, no matter how difficult things become, is usually strong enough to draw a straying family member back. Sometime, someplace, the bond of unqualified love usually becomes stronger than the forceful influences of the world.

I remember a story told by a forest ranger about a tourist who came to a national park to take pictures of wildlife. Not far from the campground he found what he was looking for—twin bear cubs rummaging around in a garbage dump, half playing, half looking for dinner. Grabbing his camera, he proceeded to take a series of pictures from a number of different angles. In his haste he failed to realize that when you find bear cubs in the forest, the mother bear is never very far away. As he moved to get a close-up shot of the playful cubs, he inadvertently came between the cubs and the mother bear, who was in the trees a short distance away. The bear struck out immediately for her cubs, and a near disaster was averted when a passerby, noticing the scene, alerted the tourist, who demonstrated unusual athletic ability as he vacated the garbage pit.

We often hear of the ferocity with which animals protect their young, and often these stories are associated with incidents about human parents who, for some unexplainable reason, abandon their children. While these actions can and should be condemned, we seem to live in a day and age when there is another kind of abandonment almost worse than a mother leaving an unwanted baby on a doorstep.

Address given at general conference October 1970.

I am talking about the temptation of parents to give up on their children when they seem to flaunt and disregard the laws of morality and conduct that the parents hold dear and that govern the home, and when the children seem to rebel against every effort parents make to correct their behavior or show them a better way.

A baby who has been left on a doorstep will be looked after by the appropriate agencies, and will usually be placed in a home where parents who want it will adopt it and love it and raise it as their own. But a boy or a girl who has been given up on by his or her parents for being off on the wrong foot, or possibly even surly and rebellious to any parental effort, is in a much more serious predicament. When the hard times come—and they will—who is going to care if the parents don't?

The tragedy of our times, as we look around us, is that we see too many young people cut adrift—some of them in trouble and some of them causing trouble for society.

Perhaps it is hard to realize that our Eternal Father also refers to these as sons and daughters; in fact, if we understand the parable of the lost sheep correctly, perhaps they are even a little more important to Him because they are not safely in the fold.

Society has given us a thousand reasons why some young people begin to rebel and wander. Yet I can't help feeling that in many cases it all must come back to those who gave them life and those who somewhere along the line gave up on them, either by deserting them or ignoring them or simply not caring enough to include their children in their lives.

I had a young girl come in to see me the other day. She was a beautiful girl, neat and clean, presenting a good appearance. But the story she told was anything but clean and far from beautiful.

From her early teenage years she had become involved in drugs. It became so bad that at one time in her life she had moved away from her family and was more or less drifting from one drug party to another. She had taken up the so-called counterculture and was high on drugs most of the time.

"Strangely enough," she said, "during all this time my father never gave up on me; and although I know I was breaking my parents' hearts, I could always go home to my father and know that he loved me and that he wouldn't condemn me as an individual, although he condemned everything I did.''

This girl went on to say that one night she had what she called a bad trip; I believe she referred to it as ''freaking out.'' She said it was such a terrifying experience that she went home to her parents and spent the rest of the night in bed with them, just as she must have done as a child when she had a nightmare. She had no real rest until her father finally gave her a blessing, which seemed to ease her mental and physical torture.

This was the turning point for her. She said she always knew her previous course was wrong but was just determined to rebel. Bit by bit she put her life back together again, and although she still has a way to go, she is going to make it now.

She had a father who never gave up on her.

Another experience comes to mind about a mother and her eighteen-year-old son, not of our faith. Let me quote her story. ''Three years ago my son made a new friend—his first link with the 'drug scene.' I tried very hard to let him know what this boy was, and to say, 'You don't need drugs in your life.' But he ignored me, and, aside from moving away, there seemed to be nothing I could do.

''As my no's became more numerous, his rejections became unbearable. One night at the dinner table he announced, 'I won't obey the rules in this house any longer.'

''He said as soon as he saved enough money, in about three months, he was going to move out. Until then, he said, 'I'm going to say what I want to say and smoke what I want to smoke.'

''I got up from the table, walked down the hall, and then came back and said, 'I've got news for you, son. Either you abide by the rules or you find a room elsewhere in three days, not three months.'

''He was shocked. But the next day he did get a job, and he soon moved out.

''Leaving home, however, did not mean giving up membership in the family. I let him know that the door was always open. I went to see his new apartment, took an interest in his new job, and invited him for a snack when he finished moving his things out. And he knew that coming home would never be interpreted as a defeat for him, but simply as a new decision.

"He had several jobs, one in a restaurant. But while he was working out problems for himself, he also was ready to put himself out to help others. Eventually he became a full-time staff member at Project Place, a center for runaways and people with drug problems.

"From time to time, he would come to see me, and I would ask him, 'How are you? Are you ready to come home?' One day he decided he was, and he moved back in. He had lost his preoccupation with drugs.

"My son has made some mistakes, experienced some pain he probably didn't have to. But I think he has come out rejecting what's wrong in the world and taking upon himself what is real and beautiful. I think a child has a right to be right, and a right to be wrong, and to know that his parents will stay with him through it all."

Perhaps you remember the story of an event that took place a few months ago. It appeared in most of the newspapers of the world. A little girl was found clinging to the fence which divides a super freeway in one of the world's largest cities. The police were summoned, and as they brought the girl to safety she unfolded a pathetic story.

It was her parents, you see, who had put her there. They had said, "Now, hang on to the fence and don't let go for any reason." Then the parents drove off—planning to desert her.

The newspaper account was graphic. You could picture the little girl, a tear in her eye, her lower lip quivering, but holding fast to the rail as cars and huge trucks went roaring by on each side, not daring to let go because her daddy had told her to hold on—standing there determined, waiting patiently for a mother and father who never intended to return.

Oh, parents, no matter what the difficulty, may we never desert our children in some dark and dangerous thoroughfare of life, no matter what prompted them to get there. When they reach the point that they need us—and for some it may be a painfully long time—I pray that we might not let them down.

> But when he was yet a great way off, his father saw him, and had compassion, and ran, and fell on his neck, and kissed him.

And the son said unto him, Father, I have sinned against heaven, and in thy sight, and am no more worthy to be called thy son.

But the father said to his servants, Bring forth the best robe, and put it on him; and put a ring on his hand, and shoes on his feet. . . .

For this my son was dead, and is alive again; he was lost, and is found. (Luke 15:20–22, 24.)

Hold Your Children's Love

The greatest trust we can gain in our lives is the trust and confidence of our children. To gain the love of our children is to enjoy one of life's greatest blessings. This should probably be at the heart of all we do for our families.

I recently attended a conference on drug abuse that was called by a group of concerned citizens. Speaking at the conference were experts in this field from throughout the United States. Their message was in accordance with that which has been echoed by almost every group investigating this problem: drug abuse is on the increase, especially among our youth.

Despite the valiant efforts of law enforcement, the availability of drugs is increasing. In fact, according to youthful offenders, drugs are readily available through what they term "the underground" in most of our intermediate and high schools.

It is evident that this is a serious problem throughout the world.

There is a great need for us, as Church members, to support efforts in our communities to strengthen law enforcement and encourage other programs designed to deal with the drug-abuse problem.

As I listened to a group of youthful former drug users, they stated that it frightens them to think that possibly as many as half of their fellow high school students might at least try drugs at some time, with a smaller number continuing on to harder drugs. These are students that evidently come from all back-

Address given at general conference April 1969.

grounds and economic levels of life. Should those young speakers be correct in their estimates, we would have to face the realization that each of our children, sometime, is going to be tempted to use drugs.

Understanding why most youthful offenders start on drugs gives us some idea as to how we might prevent this disastrous situation in our own families.

When one group who was extensively involved with drugs was asked why they started, they said without exception, "We were alienated from our parents." Somehow in their homes the love, confidence, and self-assurance that should have been conveyed from parents to children was not conveyed. Parents failed to understand the children, and the children failed to understand the parents; finally, in frustration and alienation, the children sought escape by turning to drugs.

Throughout the years, the parents had given the children many material gifts, but these gifts seemed to be in place of love instead of an expression of love.

If there is love and unity at home, and if children feel comfort there, they will know what to do when temptation presents itself. But if there is bitterness and disharmony and mistrust, then it is possible that they will seek escape through any form possible.

President David O. McKay had the following to say about the importance of example in our homes:

> I believe that parents generally are teaching their children the gospel, yet I am convinced that there is still much opportunity for improvement in this regard. I am not thinking of the set hours in which you sit down to teach these doctrines to your children, but of the example fathers and mothers give to their children regarding the faith that is dear to your hearts. Your example will teach these principles more effectively than what you say. Out of our homes come the future leaders of the government. If our homes were all they should be, the nation would be safe.

I believe the example that President McKay spoke of is most important.

It's a simple step for a young person to go from faith and love and confidence in an earthly father to faith and love and confidence in our Heavenly Father. And what better heritage can we give him than the ability to communicate with God.

From Alma we read:

> Counsel with the Lord in all thy doings, and he will direct thee for good; yea, when thou liest down at night lie down unto the Lord, that he may watch over you in your sleep; and when thou risest in the morning let thy heart be full of thanks unto God; and if ye do these things, ye shall be lifted up at the last day (Alma 37:37).

On another occasion President McKay said:

Children deserve to be taught intelligent obedience. Unhappiness in the child's life, as in the adult life, springs largely from nonconformity to natural and social laws. The home is the best place in which to develop obedience, which nature and society will later demand. . . . I do not mean getting control by cruelty, nor by foolish threats, but merely by letting the child know that he is part of a community in the home; and that the other children have their rights and each child must respect those rights.

There is the beginning of democracy, and it is in the home. (David O. McKay, *Man May Know for Himself* [Salt Lake City: Deseret Book Company, 1967], p. 299.)

And again President McKay has said: "Homes are made permanent through love. Oh, then, let love abound. If you feel that you have not the love of those little boys and girls, study to get it. Though you neglect some of the cattle, though you fail to produce good crops, ever study to hold your children's love." (*Gospel Ideals,* p. 484.)

The responsibility for communication is not alone on the shoulders of parents. The youth also have a responsibility to contribute love and strength to the family organization.

I recall a stage play which was made into a movie. It dealt with parents whose only child, a son, returned from military service. The father and the son had never been close. It was a situation where both father and son loved each other but were unable to find ways to express themselves, and therefore hostilities arose because each thought the other did not like him. Communication broke down.

But now the son was home from the army, and things were different. The father and son began to establish a whole new relationship.

The high point of the play came when the boy said to his father something like this: "Dad, I always resented you when I was younger because you never told me that you loved me. But then I realized that I had never told you that I loved you, either. Well, Dad, I'm telling you now. I love you."

For one electrifying moment the father and son embraced as the pent-up love and appreciation of years came flooding out. This would probably have never happened had the son not realized that he was as guilty of not communicating as his parents.

So young people can make a difference. They can contribute to the love in their own home by expressing their love for parents and supporting the family.

May the Lord bless us to know that it is not our material heritage that can meet and defeat this problem of drug abuse, but our spiritual heritage as expressed in the sanctity of the home and the strength of the family.

May our homes be havens of spiritual strength, and may we constantly bear witness to our children, in word and deed, of those truths that make a difference.

Man and Woman

Making the right decisions at the right time in life and learning to run the race to the end are two challenges of today's Young Special Interests. We live in a society where there are many choices. Using the divine opportunities we have to make the right choices and then making the most of our choices is essential to our happiness.

I want to talk about marriage. Before you all say, "Oh, no, not again," I want to ask you to hear me out and not make a snap decision.

My brother once told me the story of a woman who was entertaining a group of friends. She went to the kitchen to get the dessert after a very lovely meal, and she found her cat eating the dessert. Making a snap decision, she put the cat outside, smoothed over the dessert with a table knife, and served it. After the party, she found the cat in her driveway—dead. What was she to do now? After fretting for a while, she finally called all of her friends, explained the situation, and advised them to get their stomachs pumped, which they all did. The next morning her neighbor saw her and apologetically said, "I'm very sorry that I ran over your cat last night in the dark."

In the sense of that story, I hope you don't judge me too quickly.

If the Church had had Special Interests some fifteen or sixteen years ago, I would have been one of them. I had graduated from college, had spent two years on a mission and two years in

Remarks given at a Young Special Interest fireside February 1975.

the military, and I was not yet married. So I do know some of the feelings, frustrations, and thoughts that you might be having.

I want to speak to three groups tonight. First, I want to speak to the unmarried men—I can relate to you best—and then to the unmarried women. Finally, I want to speak for a few minutes to everyone.

First, to the unmarried young men may I say that as time goes on it becomes harder to make decisions about marriage. Sometimes much of the romance that characterizes a relationship when you are younger disappears when you are older. You may be waiting for a fire or a spark or some great vision to come. But let's face it; at your age it's likely not going to come that way. Sometimes we get set in our ways. Sometimes we get complacent and satisfied with the way things are, so we don't make ourselves available anymore. Sometimes we think we have special problems.

Sometimes we think the problems are financial. Jessie Evans Smith gave me a poem once about that:

> The bride, white of hair, stoops over her cane,
> Her footsteps uncertain need guiding;
> While down the church aisle,
> With a wan, toothless smile,
> The groom in a wheelchair comes riding.
>
> And who is this elderly couple thus wed?
> You will find, when you've closely explored it,
> That here is that rare,
> Most conservative pair,
> Who waited till they could afford it.
>
>   (Author unidentified)

There is something to be said about that. Some of the great experiences in marriage come from the "trial" days or the "we're-just-making-it" days or the "we-have-our-backs-against-the-wall-and-we're-trying-to-get-through" days. Anyone who would want to rob himself or his marriage of all those experiences is denying something that can indeed be a beautiful and blessed thing. If you talk to those who are very comfortable now and ask them when their best days were, they'll often declare them to be those days when they were just getting started, when they were fighting the battles and facing the crises together. Those valuable experiences can strengthen the bond of marriage and deepen love and understanding between a man and a woman.

I would like to suggest to you men tonight the way that you can get an answer from the Lord concerning marriage. If you really want an answer, there is a way you can get an answer. The problem is that sometimes we don't *want* an answer. Sometimes we expect the Lord to pick us up by the power of His Spirit and deposit us in the temple, and if He does, then we are willing to admit that we have had an answer.

The Doctrine and Covenants gives us the guidelines, but let's spell it out tonight. (Incidentally, this process is applicable to any sort of problem solving; but it is especially useful in making a decision about someone you know or are interested in, and when you want to know whether to pursue a relationship.) First, the Lord said, "study it out in your mind."

What does that mean? It means to review in your own mind the qualities of the person you know. Then put that review down on paper. Weigh it in your own mind to see if you like it and feel good about it. Be prayerful during this process, too. Is the relationship good? Am I worthy of such a person? (I had a friend who didn't get married until he was older. He said he was always looking for the perfect girl, but when he found her it didn't work out because she was looking for the perfect man.) Write down the characteristics of the person you have in mind. List the pros and cons; if you are honest, you will see both the bad traits and the good ones. There is not a soul on earth who is perfect—and the older you get the more true this becomes. Likewise, there is not a soul on earth who will find everything good about you. Life becomes more realistic as we get older.

So make your list, study it out, see if it's good. Then—and this is where many fall down—make your decision. Don't wait. You see, some people take twenty years to make a decision. They say, "Lord, tell me," and then they drift along, complaining that "I just can't get an answer." But the Lord doesn't always work that way. You must prayerfully decide what you think is the right thing to do—but you *must* come to a decision.

If you are keeping the commandments and if you are close to the Lord, you can go to Him with your decisions and say, "Father, this is what I feel you want me to do, and I'm going to proceed as if it is indeed right." If your decision is right, it will work out and you will feel a peace about the matter. If it's wrong, as long as you put it into the Lord's hands after you have made the decision, it will not work out for you. So make your decision on the best information and inspiration you have; then present the whole matter to the Lord and tell Him what you feel should be done. Then add this clause: "I'm going to proceed as if it's right; but Father, if I'm on the wrong track, then please show me that it is the wrong course." If you do that, you will begin to move in the right direction.

Now, some of the problems that some of you young men may have will probably never be ironed out until you get a loving, understanding woman by your side who is willing to accept you and begin to help you. When that happens, many of your worries will not materialize. You've had twenty or thirty years on your own now, and there is a limit to your progress as a single man. Marriage is ordained of God and there are reasons for that. It is designed so that we can help each other to exaltation and salvation. And I promise you that you can make a wise decision in this important matter if you seriously seek the Lord and are willing to act. If your decision is right, all will fall into place; and if it is wrong, you won't be able to follow through on your plans.

I made a decision about employment when I lived in Boston—a wrong decision. I went through the decision-making process, then I went to the Lord and said, "Father, I don't feel I should take this job. Therefore, I'm not going to do it, and I'm proceeding on that basis." I turned down the offer, then went through twenty-four hours of anguish. I felt terrible inside, and I knew I had made a mistake. At the end of twenty-four hours the man called me back and upped the offer. At that stage I would have probably taken the job for nothing.

I want you to know that if you want an answer—about marriage or any other facet of your life—if you are willing to study it out, make the decision, take it to the Lord, and then begin to act, you will receive an answer. Acting is often the most difficult part of this procedure.

Sometimes the image of what *might* happen beats us down so far that what *should* happen never gets a chance. When that occurs, our faith—a principle fundamental to the gospel of Jesus Christ—begins to suffer. We begin to distrust God and to even feel that He is not going to help us. That's tragic! Some in the world who do not know the gospel, who don't have the Holy Ghost or the priesthood, might be deceived into thinking this way; but certainly our knowledge of God and who we are should bolster our faith in His willingness to help us.

My early life seemed to ebb and flow. For me, it was school and a mission and the army. Then things began to level off, and I really didn't continue to move forward until the decision for marriage had been made. After that, I was in a position where I could get on with my life. Young men, as you get older, that which the Lord has called you to do or expects you to do will usually come to a standstill until you put yourself in a position for the temple-marriage covenant to be a part of your life. In other words, your progress levels off and you cannot make some important advancement until you move into this next chapter of your life.

Section 131 of the Doctrine and Covenants says: "In the celestial glory there are three heavens or degrees; And in order to obtain the highest, a man must enter into this order of the priesthood [meaning the new and everlasting covenant of marriage]; And if he does not, he cannot obtain it. He may enter into the other, but that is the end of his kingdom; he cannot have an increase." (D&C 131:1–4.) There is "no marriage or giving in marriage," no starting of mortal families out of this life.

I think if the adversary were trying to thwart the Lord's work, he would try it in two ways. First of all, realizing that these are the last days and that he the adversary is running out of time, he would try to slow things up as much as he could. If he could get the world to think, for instance, that we are going to get overpopulated, maybe he could get everyone to stop having babies. Second, he could go to those who hold the priesthood of God, and detain them from accomplishing what they were ordained to do. He would discourage them from fulfilling the marriage covenant, which covenant strengthens the kingdom by establishing solid homes and righteous families.

The Lord has much to accomplish through you and by you. Take this next step and get started. Get into the rest of your life.

There is another passage of scripture which I read quite often, and I pray that my family and I don't find ourselves in this category. It speaks of those who will inherit the terrestrial degree of glory, including Church members who "are not valiant in the testimony of Jesus" (D&C 76:79; see verses 71–80). If you interpret that statement in the context of what we are talking about tonight, it becomes a serious matter.

May the Lord bless you, young men. Make your decision; get on with the rest of your life. Don't wait for something spectacular to happen to you. The light probably won't go on. The music won't start. All of those romantic things that may have happened ten years ago will have a tendency not to happen the older you get. You become more critical. You look at people in a different light. Please understand enough of that about yourself to turn it to your own good, and make the kinds of decisions necessary so that you can get into the next phase of your life and accomplish what the Lord sent *you here* to do.

Next, may I speak to the young ladies. Sometimes it's frustrating when everyone tells you to get married and you feel you can't do anything about it. You can actually do quite a bit. But in the final analysis the decision isn't always in your hands. Perhaps in the Church we haven't put enough emphasis on running the whole race. The Lord says, "He only is saved who endureth unto the end" (D&C 53:7). In the Church we sometimes sell ourselves short on that principle. We ask, "What are your goals?" The answer is usually, "My goal is to get baptized, to go on a mission (especially for a young man), and to get married in the temple."

And then we ask, "What are the rest of your goals?" If a young woman has nothing more planned, that's not right. A young man, too, needs to set additional goals. There are some people in the Church who have achieved their basic goals: they have gone on a mission, they have married in the temple, and they have begun work in their profession. Then suddenly everything seems to fall apart in their lives, and they can't understand what has happened. Perhaps what has happened is that they have met all their goals and their life is only one-quarter over. So they become a little bit aimless, and their marriage may get into trouble because they haven't given serious thought to running the whole race.

I was at the Salt Palace in Salt Lake City two years ago with my son. We watched a new world record being set. Synchronized lights around the track flash on and off at the rate that the runners must exceed if they are to set a world's record. The spectators can follow the lights and watch runners to see how close they are to the world's record. During the 880-yard race, one runner was nearly three-quarters of a lap ahead of the light at the half-way point. At the three-quarters mark he had about a half-lap lead, and it was getting exciting. With only half a lap remaining, he gave his kick, finished strong, and left the light behind; he had set a new world record. The place went into pandemonium. It was exciting to be there.

Carrying this analogy into our lives, we can't stop just because we are ahead at the 440-yard mark if the race is an 880-yard race.

Eternal life is not gained because we have reached the 100- or the 220-yard point and we are ahead in the race. The person who attains eternal life is the person who crosses the finish line. You see, my young sisters, if all you have in mind is temple marriage and nothing else, even if you get married, your marriage might well suffer. If you don't have goals that will take you through the whole race of life, you could have some problems. If you don't get married, but you nonetheless plan to, run your race to the end, then you will find adjustment and happiness and other avenues to bring you peace of mind and satisfaction—with the understanding that ultimately, because you've kept yourself on a good course, God will withhold nothing from you.

Plan to live your life to the very end. If you get married, we're happy for you and that's wonderful. But if for any reason you don't marry, make sure that your goals don't stop at the 220 or 440 mark. Set up your life to live to the very end, and establish your goals on this basis. One of the great programs that the Church has to help you do this is the Pursuit of Excellence program. You can find much in this continuing program that will help you run the race to the end, no matter what situation you find yourself in or what your circumstances may be.

President Spencer W. Kimball has given excellent counsel about keeping yourself available in the meantime and doing the things that are necessary for you to accomplish your goals. Young ladies, your greatest enemy is probably your own apartment—especially when you stay in it all by yourselves, because it is easy to think about all the things that just aren't happening to you. Pretty soon the whole world begins to rotate around you, and all you can think about is yourself. After you do that for a while, you go to the refrigerator for escape, and then you like yourself even less.

Force yourself to get out of your apartment, if you have to. Force yourself to get into the lives of people around you who really need you. Get involved in your church and your work. Get involved in the many things that are going on around you. Find things to do. Always give yourself a little more to do than you think you can; it will keep you from sinking down into the mire of self-pity and examining everything on the basis of how it affects you. It will enable you to examine the events and circumstances of your life according to how they touch other people's lives. This is the gospel of Jesus Christ. There are some exceptional people in this church who are not married—beautiful sisters. Their lives go on. They render great service. They feel no self-pity. They have found the way. They have fashioned a life-long program that is allowing them to run the race to the end so that no single unfulfilled goal pulls them down.

So get out of your apartment; find something you can do to help other people. Sometimes you are going to have to force yourself to reach out. It's nice, sometimes, to retreat, but you have to keep yourself available. You've got to keep yourself in life, a part of life that allows the best within you to come out. Set the goals that take you out instead of keeping you home, and become involved when you don't feel like doing it. We all have to do that sometimes. I think it was Brigham Young who once said (and this is paraphrased), "Sometimes I have to say to myself, 'Get on your knees, Brigham.' " Well, sometimes you will have to say to yourself, "Look, I've got to get out of here. I've got to begin doing something for the people around me so that I can think about them instead of thinking about me." If you do that, the Lord will bless you; and when you solve that problem, you might very well put yourself in a position so that your other problems can be solved also.

Young ladies, may the Lord bless you. I hope you will all plan to run the race to the end. To you young men, may I just say that I am married to the most perfect woman there is. But there are some pretty good ones left. Let me tell you what I discovered about our own marriage.

Never is a marriage perfect at the start. That initial relationship, as far as I have been able to see, has the possibility of perfection; but it is not perfect from the beginning. If you are looking to bring into a marriage relationship everything that is perfect and ideal from day one, you will probably be disappointed. Marriages are not put together that way.

What makes a perfect marriage? Some of it is falling in love. Some of it is having the same principles, desires, and spiritual aspirations. A great deal of it is living together and striving toward a sharing, loving union. If it is going to happen, it is going to happen through the passage of years and many trials, and it is seldom perfect in the beginning. You make it that way because of the trials you go through together.

When you get married, I don't wish you any problems. But you'll have them, or the purpose of this earth experience would be wasted. Trials are not all bad. We are here to be tested. We are here to overcome. We're here to keep our lives together when things don't go the way that we want them to go. A marriage is exactly that way. Wait until your backs are against the wall and you don't know where to turn. Wait until a crisis is on top of you and you kneel down together and pray. Wait until you sit up all night with one of your children. That is what develops real love; that is what marriage is all about. A bond is forged that no one can see except you and your wife, and it's born of adversity and coming through the narrow places together. It causes you to cleave to one another as the scriptures say. There is no way that you can bring that closeness into your marriage; it comes because of the experiences that you go through together and the bond of love and unity that develops. If there is going to be a perfect marriage, it will be born of what happens to you after you're married.

I hope I haven't alienated you. Look into your own life and see where you stand, and see if you're going in the right direction. If you are not, perhaps we have touched on some principles that will help you. Maybe you have heard them before; I think you probably have. But the longer you go without taking the necessary steps, the harder it is to actually do it.

Will it be any easier next week or next month? Will it be any more right next week or next month? What are the things the Lord wants to accomplish through you? Decisions need to be made.

May I suggest a few things that may upgrade some of your goals, that may help to broaden your lives? I can't know your personal lives and you wouldn't want me to, but let me suggest some spiritual goals that will be of some use.

First, upgrade your prayers. If you don't pray night and morning, begin now. If you do so already, develop a prayerful heart (see Alma 34) and learn to follow the feelings you get in connection with your earnest prayers. That is the Spirit of the Lord, and if you learn to respond to those promptings, it will bless your life. When one of my daughters was young, she chose the busy times to ask me questions, and she was incessant. Sometimes when I was terribly busy, I didn't give her the attention that I should have and after a while she quit asking; then, when I reflected on my action and realized what I had done, I tried to get back and get involved with her again. Don't put yourself in that position with the Lord. Learn to follow the feelings that will come from your earnest prayers. Listen for the answers. I dare say these feelings come into our lives quite often, but sometimes we don't follow them. When you do follow those feelings, such actions will strengthen your faith and you will enjoy a greater outpouring of the Spirit.

The whole purpose of the gospel of Jesus Christ is to help every soul live by the Spirit of God. After the death of Joseph Smith, Brigham Young had a dream. He saw the Prophet

Joseph, who said to him, "Tell the people to learn to live by the Spirit." We can sum the whole thing up that way. If we can learn to live by the Spirit, we will begin to add dimensions to our lives that will strengthen and bless us. Every person will be a prophet for his own life.

If you receive an answer to your prayers and are not quite sure if it is the right answer, then you can do the following: Determine if it is in harmony with the teachings and principles of the Church and the living Prophet. If it is in harmony, then you can feel that you are on course. If you need further ratification, go to your priesthood leader and get his feelings. Every member of the Church has someone who presides over him or her, so we each have someone we can approach to find out if we are on course. Through this process, you can learn to live by the Holy Spirit. If you begin to cultivate it by upgrading your prayers and then learning to live by the sacred impressions that come to you in answer to the questions you are wrestling with, it will strengthen your life.

Some people say it is not possible to be perfect in this life, and in one sense that may be true. Yet it is possible for a person to cultivate the Holy Spirit and follow it to the point that he is prompted in what he does. When a person reaches that point, he knows instinctively whether his actions are offensive to the Spirit or in harmony with it. That is about as perfect as a person can get in this earthly probation, and that is one purpose of the gift of the Holy Ghost and the blessings of the gospel. It will not come overnight but we can all be growing in that direction.

My second suggestion is that you upgrade your testimony and your gospel study. If you really don't know about the gospel, find out by the influence of the Spirit. You see, that is tied to the concept of earnest prayer. If you will combine prayer and pondering with gospel study, and then build that study into your lives each day, it will help you. You will come to a knowledge of Deity. Do you want to draw near to Heavenly Father? That knowledge is available to you through the Holy Spirit and the scriptures. Begin to order your life and establish goals so that these blessings can be yours.

Finally, I can't leave you tonight without suggesting one more thing—and that is for you to serve in the mission field, if you should. I am a member of the First Quorum of the Seventy, and we have a responsibility to the missionary program of the Church. If you ought to go on a mission, you had better go, because you will find peace and fulfillment if you do. President Kimball has asked the question, "Should every young man go on a mission?" His answer is, "Yes. Every young man should go on a mission." Young ladies are not under the same obligation as the young men. If there is anyone here who should go on a mission and hasn't, pray about it. The Lord has spoken through His prophet, and his counsel is important as far as our life is concerned. If you are in your late twenties or older, then it might well be that your mission is to get married and settle down. Make plans to go on a mission later with your wife after your children are raised and have served their own missions. But if you are eligible and you haven't gone, the Lord has extended through His prophet the admonition to prepare. We pray that you will do this.

I have spoken out of the depths of my heart. There are so many things that could bless your lives, and my intent was to help you identify certain objectives so that you can begin to find your way into the avenues of life where the Lord wants you. Begin to overcome hurdles, make decisions, and build a life—a track—that you can run on to the very end, no matter what happens. If temple marriage comes, that's fine. If for any reason, young ladies, it doesn't, you will still have a meaningful, effective life because you have planned to run the race to the very end. Stay close to the Spirit; remember prayer, testimony, and gospel study. Don't become bitter or cynical; it's easy to do that sometimes, but don't let the adversary in that door or he will cause great damage. Draw close to the Lord and stay there.

I pray that the Lord will bless all of us to make inspired decisions and set righteous goals in our lives so that His Spirit might be with us.

III.
Patterns
Of Living

In the eternal pattern of things the law of the harvest prevails. Eventually all will reap what they have sown. Because of this, time is always on the side of the person who chooses to be loyal to the commandments of God.

Hanging On

There is a nobility in being able to endure to the end. Each of us has those things that come into our lives that are not of our choosing. These personal challenges are usually outside of our control, and they manage to try us and test us. The victory often comes in seeing the thing through, in enduring to the end . . . in hanging on.

I should like to salute a group of people who have developed what I believe to be a Christlike characteristic, and that is the ability to hang on. At this very moment, a good member of the Church hovers between life and death in a nearby hospital. In the last few weeks he has withstood crisis after crisis; and yet, to the amazement of all, he still hangs on. I know not whether the Lord will ordain that he should ultimately live or die at this time, but I do know there is something noble about his tenacious fight for life and his desire to hang on. Into each of our lives come these trials—trials which shake us to the very core and cause us to explore to new depths our ability to hang on.

I think of the young person who, in the quiet of the night, cannot be persuaded to compromise virtue, and decides instead to hang on, even though at the time the temptation is great.

I think of those who have withstood the test of many years, some of whom are confined and bedridden and who, in spite of the infirmity that age brings, will not give up. I see etched in the faces of these wonderful older people something of our pioneer heritage. Their lives are so filled with determination and faith,

Address given at general conference April 1974.

so filled with overcoming adversity and trial, that by their nature they simply *can't* let go.

I am reminded of two trees that were close to my home when I was growing up. One was a russian olive and grew right in our yard. It was watered every time the lawn was watered, and in that protected environment it grew to be a beautiful tree. One night a tremendous wind came up. Trees all over town were blown down, and with them went our russian olive. We had watered it so well that the roots did not have to reach far down into the soil; because those roots were so close to the surface the tree toppled over.

The second tree withstood the gale. It was a tremendous cottonwood that still stands in the lane just half a block from where I was born. This tree was in the fulness of its growth when I was a child. It has always stood by itself, completely exposed to the elements with nothing but a ditch running by, which most of the time is dry. It is gnarled and tough, and its roots have had to sink deep in order to drink of the water of life. But because its roots were forced downward, it lives. I was visiting my childhood home the other day and noticed that most of the trees around this cottonwood are gone. But, in all its power and majesty, it still hangs on.

I see in many people this same kind of beauty, wherein adversity and trial have driven the roots of faith and testimony deep in order to tap the reservoir of spiritual strength that comes from such experiences. By nature they know how to stand and fight and hang on.

My mother and my mother-in-law are characteristic of the kind of people I am talking about. One suffered a broken hip and the other underwent a severe sickness. But they have both fought back and, like so many others, are enjoying active, useful lives. When we as a family are with them, we draw strength from them and their ability to hang on in severe crises.

A few years ago, while on a mission tour in Europe, I was asked to interview a new missionary who wanted to go home. He had not been away from home before, and he was homesick and in despair in a strange country. He had actually run away once, but had come back.

I had quite a conversation with this young man. From my own missionary experience I knew something of the despair that can come into a missionary's life when he first goes into the field and begins to make his initial adjustment. If he can just hang on through those early trials, he will gradually get into the spirit of his mission and find the peace and joy that every missionary has a right to experience.

At first he was adamant in his desire to return home, but gradually the spirit of the conversation began to change. We talked about his call from a prophet. We talked about his parents' love and their desire for him to stay and succeed. We talked about those he had been called to teach.

Finally I asked, "Elder, do your father and mother want you home?"

He said no.

"Do your brothers and sisters want you home?"

He answered no.

"Does your girlfriend really want you home?"

He said, "I guess not."

I then said, "Elder, does anyone want you home right now?"

He said, "I guess not."

And then he said, with a new determination, "Brother Dunn, I think maybe I'd better try to stay." He had made a vitally important decision in his life—he had decided to hang on.

The months passed, and one day my secretary asked if I could take a minute to see a recently returned missionary. As I walked out of my office to greet my visitor, I saw this same missionary. I didn't recognize him at first; he seemed taller because he was standing straight. Unlike the first time, he looked me right in the eye and his whole countenance was smiling. I can't remember what we talked about, but I shall never forget his image. He was going home now, a servant of the Lord, having completed an honorable mission. His roots were reaching downward, and although there will be the usual trials ahead, he knows something of what it means to hang on for a while longer when everything looks its blackest.

I don't know all the reasons why the Lord tries us in this life, but there are two or three that come to mind. First, I think He wants to know whom He can trust. The Lord found He could trust Abraham because he was willing to offer his own son as a sacrifice in obedience to the Lord's commands. Many thought that Zion's Camp was a tragic waste of time, until it was later demonstrated that the Lord used this ordeal to find whom He could trust. He wanted to know who had roots of faith and testimony that reached deep into the ground, and who had such shallow roots that the first wind of adversity would blow them over.

Second, the Lord tells us in the Doctrine and Covenants that adversity came to Joseph Smith to give him experience (see D&C 122:7). There is something about life's eternal purpose that requires us to meet and experience trial and sorrow as we seek to overcome, "for if they never should have bitter they could not know the sweet" (D&C 29:39).

Third, I believe that only through such experiences can a person develop true charity, the pure love of Christ.

We read the following from Moroni in the Book of Mormon:

> If a man be meek and lowly in heart, and confesses by the power of the Holy Ghost that Jesus is the Christ, he must needs have charity; for if he have not charity he is nothing; wherefore he must needs have charity.
>
> And charity *suffereth long,* and is kind, and envieth not, and is not puffed up, seeketh not her own, is not easily provoked, thinketh no evil, and rejoiceth not in iniquity but rejoiceth in the truth, *beareth all things,* believeth all things, hopeth all things, *endureth all things.*
>
> Wherefore, my beloved brethren, if ye have not charity, ye are nothing, for charity never faileth. Wherefore, cleave unto charity, which is the greatest of all, for all things must fail—
>
> But charity is the pure love of Christ. (Moroni 7:44–47; emphasis added.)

May I say, then, to those who are now or will be facing deep trials: May the Lord bless you that you may continue to hang on. There is purpose in it all, and He has promised us that the severity of our trials will not be greater than we can endure. As the words of the hymn tell us,

When through fiery trials thy pathway shall lie,
My grace, all sufficient, shall be thy supply.
The flame shall not hurt thee, I only design
Thy dross to consume and thy gold to refine.
("How Firm a Foundation," *Hymns,* no. 66, verse 5.)

And finally, this promise from the Master: "And again, be patient in tribulation until I come; and, behold, I come quickly, and my reward is with me, and they who have sought me early shall find rest to their souls" (D&C 54:10).

Called of God

In the gospel of Jesus Christ, a higher law is followed in rendering Church service. It is not a matter of being elected by peers or taking turns filling a position. In the Church a man serves because he is called of God.

Sustaining general officers of the Church is part of the revealed procedure which takes place from the general to the ward or branch level, and which allows every member the opportunity of sustaining a person who has been called to office. Sustaining, however, should not be confused with voting into office.

Joseph Smith clearly described how a person is called to a position in The Church of Jesus Christ of Latter-day Saints: "We believe that a man must be called of God, by prophecy, and by the laying on of hands by those who are in authority, to preach the Gospel and administer in the ordinances thereof" (Articles of Faith 1:5).

When we sustain officers, we are given the opportunity of sustaining those whom the Lord has already called by revelation. The dictionary tells us that the word *sustain* means to bear up, to support, to furnish sustenance for, to aid effectually, to hold valid, to confirm or corroborate. The Lord gives us the opportunity to sustain the action of a divine calling or express ourselves if for any reason we may feel otherwise. To sustain is to make the action binding on ourselves and to commit support to those people whom we have sustained.

When a person goes through the sacred act of raising his arm to the square, he should remember with soberness that which he

---

Address given at general conference April 1972.

has done and should act in harmony with his sustaining vote, both in public and in private. If for any reason we have a difficult time sustaining those in office, then we are to go to our local priesthood leaders and discuss the issue with them and seek their help.

Brigham Young, when speaking of Joseph Smith, made the following statement:

> Who called Joseph Smith to be a prophet? Did the people or God? God, and not the people called him. Had the people gathered together and appointed one of their number to be a prophet, he would have been accountable to the people; but inasmuch as he was called by God, and not the people, he is accountable to God only and the angel who committed the gospel to him, and not to any man on earth. The Twelve are accountable to the prophet, and not to the Church for the course they pursue. (*History of the Church*, 5:521–22.)

And then, of course, it was added that all members are accountable to the principles and teachings of the gospel.

If we are to take that same principle and apply it at the ward level, we can see that the bishop, who is considered the father of his ward and who leads his ward with judiciousness, love, patience, and kindness, is nonetheless not answerable to the members of his ward, but instead is answerable to the Lord and to those priesthood leaders who preside over him. The bishop is answerable *for* the members of his ward, but not necessarily *to* the members of his ward.

The Church of Jesus Christ, then, is organized from the top down. In contrast, the usual man-made organizations are organized from the bottom up. In this Church, the Lord raised up a prophet first; and then, through the holy priesthood and the power of revelation, He revealed the organization and structure of His Church from the highest to the least. While the Lord gives us the opportunity of sustaining that which He has revealed, this does not constitute voting someone into office; instead, it is properly referred to as the law of common consent. In contrast, a man-made organization will establish its own laws by the vote of its membership.

With the Church and kingdom of God organized from the top down by the power of revelation, Jesus Christ Himself can stand at the head and lead His own church through His Apostles and prophets.

There are many in the Church who may not be as attentive to their duties as they might be—not because they haven't been called of God by revelation, but because they did not fully realize that fact when they were called. Let me refer again to the fifth article of faith: "We believe that a man must be called of God, by prophecy, and by the laying on of hands by those who are in authority, to preach the Gospel and administer in the ordinances thereof."

A calling in the Church is both a personal and a sacred matter, and everyone is entitled to know that he or she has been called to act in the name of God in that particular position. Every person in this Church has the right to know that he has been called of God. If he does not have that assurance, then I would suggest that he give his calling serious, prayerful consideration so that he can receive what he has a right to receive. Further, if a priesthood leader realizes that there are those under his stewardship who may not have this clear understanding, he can do something about it. He cannot call them again, but he can bring them in and reassure them of the divine nature of their calling.

I am most grateful for the great leaders of the Church who have helped me to feel and understand the divine nature of the callings I have received over the years. I can't ever remember coming away from a personal discussion with a priesthood leader who was delivering a call to me without feeling in my heart the realization and assurance that I had been called of God, and that that priesthood leader was a servant of the Lord and was acting in his own office and calling.

When I was first sustained as a General Authority, the sustaining was preceded by a divine calling from a prophet. When I left President David O. McKay's office that morning, as inadequate as I felt, I knew that I had been called of God by revelation; and the Spirit confirmed again something that I already knew—that President McKay was a prophet of God, and that this, the Lord's Church, is led by Apostles and prophets who are divinely guided.

What a marvelous thing it would be if throughout the Church, after the inspiration was received and worthiness determined, priesthood leaders would take the time to create the right atmosphere for a holy and divine calling to be extended in keeping with the fifth article of faith. Such a calling, I suspect, would emphasize the fact that the priesthood leader was delivering a call from the Lord. Then, if in the future we were asked, "Who called you?" our immediate response would be to say with conviction, "The Lord Jesus Christ," and secondly to say, "But the call was delivered through Bishop Jones or Stake President Green." Perhaps in too many cases that gets reversed, and when we answer the question "Who called you?" we mention only the name of Bishop Jones.

The Prophet Joseph Smith taught: "All the ordinances, systems, and administrations on the earth are of no use to the children of men, unless they are ordained and authorized of God; for nothing will save a man but a legal administrator; for none others will be acknowledged either by God or angels" (*History of the Church,* 5:259). Let me repeat that last part: "For nothing will save a man but a legal administrator; for none others will be acknowledged either by God or angels."

It is my testimony that when we raise our hands to sustain a prophet, seer, and revelator, we also sustain a legal administrator in the teachings and ordinances of the gospel of Jesus Christ; and because we have a prophet standing at our head, that which is done under his direction throughout the Church is binding not only on earth but in heaven. The fact that we have Apostles and prophets, and that we have the opportunity to sustain Apostles and prophets, allows us to do those things which will reach into eternity and guarantee our eternal salvation. Indeed, any man who will listen and who will humble himself before the Lord is guaranteed the opportunity to receive those ordinances and blessings which allow him entrance into the kingdom of God.

I testify that the Apostles and prophets whom we have sustained receive revelation from God for the ongoing work of the kingdom in this day. May the Lord so bless us now that we may sustain those whom He has called, and do that which is divinely expected of us.

The Flower of Purity

There is a refreshing beauty and strength in those who are pure.
True freedom comes from such purity and opens the windows of
heaven.

There is also a purity that comes to the truly repentant, to
those who have gone through remorse, have repented, and have
appealed to the Father for forgiveness.

The Lord has told us that he has put us on earth that we
might have joy. This is not pleasure as the world understands it,
but is joy. Our Heavenly Father created us; because He is our
creator, He knows us best of all. He knows what brings us sad-
ness. He also knows what we will have to do in order to return to
His presence and live with Him. This is the reason why He has
given to us the gospel of Jesus Christ and its commandments.
All of this is to help us prepare ourselves so that we can return to
our Father in Heaven and live where He lives and feel comfortable in His presence.

The world does not understand this, and most people
usually seek after the pleasures of the world. But these pleasures never last, and many times they bring unhappiness, pain,
and misery. The world looks for joy that lasts, but they try to
find it in pleasures that violate the commandments of God, and
they will never find any true happiness there.

When I think of the joy that comes from keeping the commandments of our Father in Heaven, I think of the beautiful

Address given at Papeete Tahiti Area Conference, Mother-Daughter session, March
1976.

flowers here in this meeting and which grow in abundance throughout these islands. The Lord tells us to "consider the lilies of the field, how they grow; they toil not, neither do they spin: And yet I say unto you, That even Solomon in all his glory was not arrayed like one of these." (Matthew 6:28–29.)

If one studies one of these blossoms, he can see that it is beautifully formed and that its colors are rich and expressive. There is a softness to the touch and a purity that is unmistakable. And the fragrance that comes from these blossoms makes them all the more beautiful.

Have you ever seen an artificial flower? At first glance, they look like real flowers; but they give up no lovely fragrance, and when one touches an artificial flower it becomes quite clear that it is not the real thing.

Oh, may all mothers and daughters seek after the blossoms of true joy–the joy that our Father in Heaven speaks about. Sometimes the world will place before us the artificial flower of worldly pleasure and try to make us think that it is true joy. But that kind of flower can give no fragrance of its own, nor can it bring any lasting happiness.

Virtue is like the beautiful flowers that blossom throughout these islands. They are lovely to behold. They are delicate, and they are a blessing to all those who see them and enjoy their fragrance.

Immorality is like the artificial flower. The adversary would like to make people think that it is as good as the real flower of virtue; but it is not and never can be, and only leads to disappointment and heartbreak.

Concerning immorality, the prophet Alma wrote, "Know ye not, my son, that these things are an abomination in the sight of the Lord; yea, most abominable above all sins save it be the shedding of innocent blood or denying the Holy Ghost?" (Alma 39:5.) From this scripture we learn that the sin of immorality is extremely serious and ranks only behind the shedding of innocent blood and denying the Holy Ghost. And the Lord has said that we must "neither commit adultery, nor kill, *nor do anything like unto it*" (D&C 59:6; emphasis added), which has reference to the immoral acts that lead up to serious transgressions.

In his book *The Miracle of Forgiveness,* Spencer W. Kimball quoted David O. McKay as follows:

> Please young folk, preserve your virtue. . . . Do not tamper with sin . . . , do not permit yourselves to be led into temptation. Conduct yourselves seemly and with due regard, particularly you young boys, to the sanctity of womanhood. Do not pollute it. (Spencer W. Kimball, *The Miracle of Forgiveness* [Salt Lake City: Bookcraft, 1969], p. 63.)

Later in this book, President Kimball reminded us that "the sin of fornication is well known, and the scriptures from beginning to end decry this act of defilement" (p. 64). He continued:

> Many rationalize that this attraction of two unmarried people is love, and they seek thereby to justify their intimate relations. This is one of the most false of all of Satan's lies. It is lust, not love, which brings men and women to fornication and adultery. No person would injure one he truly loves, and sexual sin can only result in injury (p. 65).

President Kimball pointed out that regardless of what the world says, The Church of Jesus Christ of Latter-day Saints must continue to fortify its people against sin and to stand firm for total fidelity.

From the revelations of the Lord and from the writings of all of the prophets, it is clear that virtue is a quality which, when practiced by the children of the Lord, causes Him to smile down upon them and pour out blessings upon them. Mothers, continue to teach this great quality to your daughters and to your sons, not alone as a principle that you would like to have them practice, but as a principle that the Lord God has revealed again and again that He would have them practice, and that every prophet since the world began has outlined as the only way a person can return to the presence of God.

You beautiful young girls, keep yourselves clean. Bring trust and confidence into the marriage you hope to have by keeping yourselves virtuous. The Lord has made it clear that in His kingdom there is no other way. If some have to go through the remorse and pain of repentance, let it happen now. How much better it is, however, to keep the commandments and to be virtuous so that the painful process of repentance is not necessary.

The teaching of morality and virtue to your sons, mothers, can help to prepare them for missionary service. There are quite a number of missionaries serving at this time, and they are doing a fine job. We need a great many more, however, in order to accomplish the Lord's work. If they are brought up worthy to go, and if they are encouraged to go by their mothers and fathers and by their sisters and girlfriends, then it is easier for them to answer the call of the Lord and to teach the gospel to those who are yet in darkness. Mothers and daughters can have a great and positive influence on the young men of the Church by encouraging them to answer the call of the Lord and to serve in the mission field.

Oh, mothers and daughters alike, may your lives be like the beautiful flowers, fresh and pure and rich to the eye of the beholder, giving off beautiful fragrances and by their very existence demonstrating the beauty and majesty and love of the Creator.

The Pioneer Spirit

There were far more pioneers than those who crossed the plains to settle the Salt Lake Valley. In virtually every country where the gospel has been proclaimed, there are those who have gone through hardship and sacrifice for the gospel of Jesus Christ. In their own right, they are no less pioneers than those first settlers who arrived in Salt Lake Valley. The call to build Zion wherever we are is creating new opportunities and challenges and a new brand of pioneer with each generation.

I would like to spend a few moments talking about pioneers. Not the pioneers that crossed the mountains and plains of the United States to settle Salt Lake City, but a hardy band of Polynesian pioneers. Some were Samoan, many were Hawaiian, and there were also some Maoris.

They established a colony or village in Skull Valley, Tooele County, Utah, in 1889. How these faithful Saints from the islands of the sea came to establish a colony in the middle of the desert, and how they overcame their difficulties and hardships to make a success of the colonization plan, is one of the most remarkable and interesting chapters to be found in our Church history.

I know there are people in this meeting today who are directly related to these pioneers from Polynesia. Some of our Saints in Sauniatu are related to these pioneers, and others from different villages are also related.

Address given at Apia Samoa Area Conference February 1976.

The colony was called Iosepa, which means Joseph. This was in honor of the sixth president of the Church, Joseph F. Smith, who had served as a missionary among the Hawaiians and was solicitous of their welfare. The citizens of Iosepa came to Utah in the late 1800s as part of the great gathering movement carried on by the Church during its early years of existence. They also came so they could do their temple work and take advantage of the ordinances of the temple. This gathering movement is, of course, no longer required of the Saints. In fact, the Presidency of the Church have advised the Saints to stay where they are and build up Zion in their own country and among their own people. And, with temples being constructed throughout the world, it is no longer necessary for the Saints to go all the way to Salt Lake City to enjoy the temple ordinances.

At first these early Polynesian pioneers settled around Warm Springs in the northwest part of Salt Lake City. But as time went on and their numbers increased, there was a need for a permanent home—a place where they could have employment and enjoy their Polynesian way of life.

On May 16, 1889, a committee of three was appointed by the First Presidency to look for such a place. The Polynesians appointed three to serve with this committee, and they began to inspect numerous farms and ranches offered for sale throughout Utah. They finally settled on the ranch of John T. Rich in Skull Valley, Tooele County. The property consisted of 1,920 acres, with twelve miles of substantial wire fence. Also purchased from Rich were 129 horses and 335 head of horned cattle. With the help of the Church the Iosepa Agricultural and Stock Company was organized, and the property was bought on installments. It was to be a cooperative community with everyone working on the various projects undertaken by the community, and each worker was paid for his labors.

The village was organized and the head of each family drew lots to determine where in the village they would settle. If a lot suited the person who drew it, he could buy the title to the land for between twenty-four and seventy-five dollars. Each lot had sufficient room for a home, a garden, a barn, and corral facilities for livestock. The company held all the lands and livestock of the colony, except for the lots purchased by colonists and the teams of riding horses owned by individuals.

Iosepa was seventy-five miles west of Salt Lake City. The time designated for the move was August 26, 1889. The departing Polynesians were served a huge feast by the bishops of the Nineteenth and Twenty-second wards in Salt Lake City prior to their departure. They made part of the journey by train, but most of it had to be made by teams and wagons that were provided by the Tooele Stake. There was an overnight stay at Grantsville, a small community halfway between Iosepa and Salt Lake. On August 28, this group of Polynesian pioneers reached the place that was to be the Utah home of the Polynesian Latter-day Saints for the next twenty-eight years. It was declared Pioneer Day, and in the evening a meeting was held that included songs, prayers, and speeches of thanksgiving. The brethren from Tooele Stake participated in the activities.

Iosepa was an unlikely place for Saints from the South Sea Islands to settle. Unlike the beautiful greenery and lush vegetation of their native homes, Skull Valley was a wilderness. The only people living in the valley were a few homesteaders and a tribe of Indians. The only thing that grew naturally was sagebrush; with some difficulty this had to be cleared before any crops could be planted. Skull Valley was very cold in the winter and very hot in the summer. As much as three or four feet of snow might be on the ground in the winter; the temperature would be as low as zero, keeping the snow from melting until some time in the spring. In the summer there was almost no rain, and the sun beating down on the bleak desert would sometimes send the temperatures up to a hundred degrees and cause the air to be very dry. A one-hour heavy rainstorm in Samoa would cause more water to fall than a year of rain in Iosepa. Because of this, the pioneers had to build ditches and bring water down from the mountain streams so they could water their crops and their cattle and horses.

There would be absolutely nothing that one could compare between the beautiful islands of the sea and the arid desert known as Skull Valley.

In the original group were 45 to 50 Polynesians, and at one time the colony had a population of 228 people.

The first years were hard ones and required a great deal of adjustment. Such familiar food staples as taro root would not grow, so wheat flour was substituted. Seafood, of course, was not available. They were, however, able to plant carp, a certain kind of fish, in some of the small marshy ponds near the town. Their fondness for pork did not change, and they found that they could raise pigs in Skull Valley (and many were raised).

Those early years were hard. Being isolated, the pioneers had to establish a community that would support itself. In the beginning they sold feed to men who raised cattle and sheep in the area, and they also fed these cattle and sheep during the winter months for a certain price. Later, the community bought cattle and sheep to fatten and sell. Another successful venture was the raising of hogs for market. Eventually the colony established a successful general store. Not only did members of the colony trade at the general store, but homesteaders from throughout the valley would also come and trade.

A few years after the village was established, leprosy struck. This and other diseases took the lives of many pioneers; however, gradually they overcame this and health in the village became generally good.

One of the high points in the history of Iosepa was in 1892 as the Salt Lake Temple was nearing completion. Additional funds were needed to finish construction of the temple, and the Church established Sunday, May 1, as a special fast day during which donations would be collected to complete the temple. In Iosepa, a special meeting lasted from 10:00 A.M. to 2:00 P.M., after which each of the Polynesian colonists made a donation. A total of fourteen hundred dollars was collected. Early the next year the temple was completed, and the Polynesian Saints thereafter made regular trips to this sacred edifice.

In spite of the hardship, the citizens of Iosepa were a happy people; and, in keeping with their customs, they established musical groups. Among these were the Glee Club, which was a young men's choral group, and the Iosepa Troubadors and Orchestra, consisting of a number of native and other instruments. These groups would perform at such celebrations as Pioneer Day, which was celebrated on August 28, the day the Polynesian Saints first arrived to establish Iosepa. New Year's and Christmas were celebrated with a mixture of Polynesian and Western activities. It was not unusual for General Authorities of the Church from Salt Lake City and Church leaders from Tooele County to come and celebrate some of these holidays with the citizens of Iosepa.

During its twenty-eight years of existence, Iosepa grew from an isolated, struggling settlement to a well-established colony that was gradually able to support itself. The town was laid out in an orderly fashion and homes were built. Trees, rosebushes, and shrubs were planted, and truly the desert had begun to blossom as a rose.

In 1915, however, President Joseph F. Smith, after returning from one of his frequent trips to the Hawaiian Islands, made the announcement that a temple would be built at Laie, Oahu. The main reason for the Polynesian Saints' colonization of Iosepa was so they could be close to a temple. Now one was being built in the Islands, and the Saints from the South Seas would no longer have to come such a great distance. With the blessing of the Church, they gradually began to move back to the islands of the sea. By 1917, Iosepa was no more. It had been a bright star in the history of the Church, but had served its purpose.

Last summer I took my family to visit what was left of Iosepa. We drove out past Grantsville and into Skull Valley along the same route that the original band of Polynesian pioneers had traveled some eighty-five years ago. There is virtually nothing left of the colony. The buildings have been torn down. Sagebrush and other growth have covered over the once well-kept lots and streets. The trees are gone, and only an occasional tangled rose bush serves as a reminder of the once beautiful community that has been swallowed up by the desert.

We walked to a small rise in the northeast section of the old village and came upon the graveyard. A fence had been built around it, but it had suffered the effects of time and the hostile desert climate. There are some fifty Polynesians buried there, including those who first breathed the breath of life in the land of Samoa. It was sad to look across the sagebrush valley on that warm summer day and realize that these were the ones who were left behind. There were no grandchildren or great-grandchildren to tend the graves, no one to leave a flower in memory of a departed soul.

Iosepa stands for the Polynesian pioneers—those who were willing to struggle and work together and sacrifice because of their testimonies of the gospel of Jesus Christ.

Iosepa stands for the importance of temple ordinances. It stands for those who were willing to give up everything in order that they could go into the temple of the Lord and save themselves and their dead ancestors.

Iosepa stands for the true pioneer spirit that was part of the foundation for The Church of Jesus Christ of Latter-day Saints in these last days.

Iosepa stands for the realization that the Lord, through His prophets, requires us to do different things at different times in order to meet the needs of building the kingdom of God on the earth. At one time there was a day of gathering in the Church, and all were asked to come to the western United States as part of this gathering. That day is no longer. Just as Iosepa disappeared when temples were built closer to the Polynesian people, so the leaders of the Church have told us that there is no longer a reason to gather to America.

Instead, they have asked us to be a light unto our fellowmen in our own country and among our own people. If we are to build the gospel of the kingdom in Samoa, we must do it by living here and being a good example. We cannot be a light on the hill to guide other people if the people we are to help and influence are here and we are off in a foreign land. The Lord, through His prophets, has told us to stay where we are and to build Zion.

May we spend our days in teaching our children the gospel of Jesus Christ and keeping them close to us. May we show our fellowmen that this Church truly is the kingdom of God upon the face of the earth. And when this life is over, may our children and grandchildren mourn our departure and bury us in a place where loved ones will remember, next to our own parents and the members of our family. And when that great resurrection morning comes, may we come forward, not in a strange place, but among our family and friends.

Time Is on Your Side

Although we may not perceive any justice when those who violate divine laws seem to do it with impunity and without any ill effects, in the eternal pattern of things the law of the harvest prevails. Eventually all will reap what they have sown. Because of this, time is always on the side of the person who chooses to be loyal to the commandments of God.

I knew an athlete some years ago who had tremendous talent. He had almost perfect physical coordination. In fact, he was so good he would not train, and yet still exceeded the talents and abilities of those around him. It was demoralizing sometimes for those who had to follow every training rule in order to bring themselves to a peak of physical performance, only to have him exceed them because of his natural abilities.

But I happened to be present at the stadium one afternoon a few years later when this athlete, who had progressed rather rapidly in a very promising sports career, had what some would call his moment of truth.

He was now playing with people who had talents as great as his, and as the pace of the game picked up, the pressures began to mount. He reached inside himself for that great second effort that he had always been able to pull out; but it became obvious that this time he could not marshal all he needed.

That afternoon marked the beginning of a gradual decline which finally found him retiring from the game years before he

---

Address given at general conference October 1969.

should have retired. His original decision to disregard the rules of preparation had, in the end, cost him many years of performance and pleasurable rewards.

Many times we see people around us who violate the patterns of living and the rules that we have been taught to live by, and they seem to do it without any ill effects. On the surface, it may seem that it makes no difference whether we live these rules, because those who violate them appear to suffer no consequences.

In all ages there have been challenges to those who believe in virtue, honesty, and high moral standards—challenges to those who accept these standards as God-given and believe that they will ultimately carry their own reward.

"We are always in the forge, or on the anvil," said Beecher. "By trials God is shaping us for higher things."

These challenges come from many different directions. For instance, there are those who expound the so-called new morality and say that it matters not if a person participates in free love, nor does the marriage contract mean that husband and wife should be faithful to each other. But those who believe this are wrong; and time, which is running out on them if they don't change, will prove them wrong.

"There are some things which never grow old-fashioned," said President David O. McKay. "The sweetness of a baby is one. The virtue and chastity of manhood is another. Youth is the time to lay the foundation for our homes. I know there are those who tell you that suppression is wrong, but I assure you that self-mastery, not indulgence, is the virtue that contributes to the virility of manhood and the beauty of womanhood." (*Man May Know for Himself* [Salt Lake City: Deseret Book Co., 1967], p. 250.)

There are also those who sanction the use of illicit drugs, reasoning that they are so widely used they should be accepted and even condoned; for, they say, they create no more problems than alcohol. Those who use this reasoning fail to point out, however, that in the United States alone alcohol disables over six and one-half million people each year, and that over one-half of the fatal traffic accidents are related to excessive drinking.

To recommend the use of drugs by comparing them to alcohol is like approving of a hepatitis epidemic on the basis that it probably won't be any more damaging than tuberculosis.

There has been sharp divergence of opinion in the United States over the use of these drugs—so much so that it prompted the organization of a presidential task force a few years ago to ferret out the facts. This task force, in its initial report, indicated that the widespread use of marijuana represents a significant mental health problem. Depending on the dose, it may have detrimental effects on both the mental and physical well-being of the user. Because of these perils, the report continued, every effort should be made by the federal government to curb the import and distribution of marijuana as well as stronger drugs. (See *Christian Science Monitor,* September 15, 1969.) More recent studies tend to support these findings.

When you are challenged by others because you believe in the law of chastity, because you believe that drugs are not the answer, because you believe in such God-given axioms as "Thou shalt not steal" and "Thou shalt not lie," or because you have a simple and basic faith in God the Father and in His Son Jesus Christ and in your own eternal worth—when you meet such challenges, just remember that time is on your side. Be patient, and the same people who challenge you, if they do not change, will ultimately prove to you by their lives that they don't have the answers—either for you or for themselves.

This is not to say that your task will be easy. Sometimes the desire to be accepted by an individual or a group causes a person to do things that he really doesn't want to do. But if you can maintain your integrity, you'll come to understand what Lehi meant when he taught that "Men are, that they might have joy" (2 Nephi 2:25)—not fleeting pleasure, but real joy.

Beware of the temptation to violate God's laws with the thought in mind that you can always repent, without really anticipating any remorse as a result of the wrongdoing.

Repentance is a great principle, probably the greatest in the gospel of Jesus Christ; thank heaven the Lord holds the opportunity of repentance out to all. Yet perhaps we should occasionally reflect on the awful nature of sin, rather than relying continually on the redeeming qualities of repentance.

We have three daughters whom we love very dearly. When the oldest was three years old, I was doing some studying at my desk at home. She was in the room playing with a glass of water that was on the desk.

As she picked up the large glass with her little fingers, I repeatedly warned her that she must be careful or she would drop the glass—which, of course, she finally did. It shattered as it hit the floor, and glass splinters went in every direction.

Showing the patience of a wise parent, I immediately spanked her, explaining to her that the spanking was the consequence of her insisting on not listening to me and picking up the glass until it dropped and was broken. She shed some tears and gave me a hug (which she usually did when she knew she was in trouble) and the event was soon forgotten.

Since she often plays in her bare feet, I took her out of the room and made every effort to sweep up all the glass particles. But the thought came to me that perhaps I hadn't gotten all the splinters of glass; at some future time, those little feet might find the splinters that went undetected, and she would have to suffer anew for what she had done.

For a young person to violate the law of chastity or some other commandment, and then later to put his or her life in order, will require the forgiveness of an understanding and loving God. Yet as that person progresses in life and reaches a point when he or she enters into a marriage contract, and as he has children of his own, it just might be that a splinter of a previous wrongdoing somewhere on the floor of his life might prick his conscience. This is not to say that the Lord hasn't forgiven the person. But as he begins to understand the full meaning, the full significance of what he once did, he unfortunately may find it difficult to forgive himself. Perhaps this is ultimately the hardest part of repentance, being able to forgive oneself in light of the seriousness of the transgression. Certainly in this, as in all other things, we need the Lord's help.

It is my testimony that the teachings of the Church of Jesus Christ are for the purpose of saving all mankind from the remorse of wrongdoing. Time is on the side of those who hold to these principles and is working against those who do otherwise.

Heritage

Our heritage as Latter-day Saints includes the Lord's dealings with us as individuals, as families, and as a Church. We ought to guard and treat this heritage with reverence, preserving it and passing it on to those who come after us to show what great things the Lord has done. Thus, one means of building faith is to keep our heritage alive in the hearts of each generation.

I'd like to share a little about my own life. I was born and raised in Tooele. There are a few other General Authorities who have some relationship to Tooele. President J. Reuben Clark was born and raised in Grantsville, which is about seven miles from Tooele. While the two towns really don't claim each other, they're close enough so that the competition is strong. Elder LeGrand Richards spent a number of his early years in Tooele. His father, as I recall, was a counselor in the stake presidency there before he was called into the Quorum of the Twelve. I like to talk to Elder LeGrand Richards because he knew my grandfather and my grandmother, and I never had the opportunity of being acquainted with either of them. He recalls for me from time to time some experiences of my own heritage.

I would like to share with you a few of the experiences I had in my hometown of Tooele. Some people say, and I think erroneously, that the blessings of the gospel and the inspiration and direction of the Spirit as they existed at the time of the restoration of the gospel are not among us today as much as they were

Remarks given at the Washington Temple dedication November 1974 and at a Brigham Young University devotional May 1982.

at an earlier time. It has been my experience that, as the Church grows bigger, the blessings of the gospel and spiritual experiences are as available to us now as they ever were.

My father was called as stake president when I was fairly young. In those days stake presidents were not called for only a few years—my father served for twenty years as president of the Tooele Stake. He had some great experiences associated with that service. He was called when I was six and released when I was twenty-six. I think it was Elder Joseph F. Merrill, a member of the Quorum of the Twelve, who called him. He told of going down the list of priesthood leaders in the stake and coming to the name of my father and feeling, as it were, an electric shock. This was before he had met him. Later, in telling this experience, he said he also heard a voice that indicated to him that this was the person who should be called as president of the Tooele Stake.

The whole story becomes, to our family anyway, a little more significant when we reflect on the fact that, before my father was born, his mother passed away. She recorded in her diary and told her children of passing through the veil and being met by her loved ones and family and having them tell her that it was not time for her to come there yet. They said she needed to bring another child into the world, a child who would play a significant role in the building of the kingdom. In this way she would fill the measure of her probation.

My grandmother tells some interesting things associated with this experience. She was given the opportunity, of course, to come back. She was told that if she did come back she must again feel pain. She told how pleasant and peaceful it was to cross beyond the veil; on the other hand, she said that it was painful to come back. I've often reflected on that. You know, sometimes we're prone because of our love and anxiety for people to anguish over them and try to intercede on their behalf as they hover between life and death. How wise it is for us to allow the Lord to accomplish for a person what He will accomplish rather than in every case to ask that our loved one may be kept on or held in mortality. I know in some cases we keep them on in pain rather than allow them to go in peace.

She also said there were people a short distance from her

who couldn't come to her, and she couldn't go to them. She recognized them from her native Scotland. They called to her when they knew that she was going to return from beyond the veil. "When you go back, please have someone do our work for us," they said. "Have someone do our temple work for us." Sometimes I think we look upon the programs of the Church as duties that just keep us busy. We don't always realize that they are indeed a part of eternity, that specific things bring blessings to specific people, and that it is important for us to be involved in the work of the gospel.

A number of months after that experience, my father was born. When he was a teenager his mother passed away—permanently this time. Later, during his mission in Oklahoma, he was called as a conference president and served for a time without a companion because there were an odd number of missionaries. During this time he was stricken with influenza and became delirious while by himself in the backroads of Oklahoma. Fortunately, somone took him in although they didn't know who he was. They laid him down in a corner of their little cabin, and there he hovered between life and death.

Back home his sister was also stricken. She tells of passing through a night of extreme crisis during which their mother came to her and told her that she would be all right. Then she said, "I must hurry back to your brother in the mission field, who is in need of me." Then she was gone. Father always said he knew he was never alone as he served his mission.

My mother's great-grandmother, who resided in Long Island, had a dream one night. She saw two men who were coming to preach the gospel of Jesus Christ. The next day Orson Hyde and his companion (now believed to be Parley P. Pratt) knocked on their door. They were immediately recognized as the men in my great-great-grandmother's dream and were invited into the home. Because of this, Jacob Brower and Phoebe Pearsall Brower became the first converts of the Church in South Hempstead, Long Island.

I learn from these experiences that we don't always understand that a calling in the Church, no matter to whom or where it comes or where the person is to serve, is fundamentally and basically a divine matter. "We believe a man must be called of

God, by prophecy'' (Articles of Faith 1:5). We believe that this is the gospel of Jesus Christ and that the Savior directs His own church. The reality of the divine nature of a person's call is very significant to me because of some of these experiences.

Let me tell you another experience about a friend of mine. His name was Robbie Shields. He'll never go down in the annals of history as one of the great men of the world—only a few people knew him in the Church. The thing that Robbie Shields had going for him was that the Lord loved him. Robbie Shields lived next door to me in his later life. As my brother and I were growing up, first he was my brother's senior home teaching companion, and then he was mine—always faithful, always there, always a word of prayer before we went out, always taking care of the duties of a home teacher with faithfulness and loyalty, always helping us to do our job as Aaronic Priesthood bearers and home teachers.

I can remember sitting in the Tooele First Ward on many occasions on fast Sunday and listening to Robbie, who would always sit on the north side halfway back, tell of the experience of how the Lord spoke to him. In his younger days he taught a Sunday School class, and they were looking for an answer to one of their questions. He prayed and searched and read and prayed and searched and read.

One day he was out hauling hay in Pine Canyon. He was by himself forking the hay onto the wagon when a voice spoke to him, calling him by name.

He said to the voice, ''Who are you?'' and the voice said, ''I am the Lord.''

Robbie Shields said, ''Why can't I see you?''

The voice said, ''Because you don't have to.''

That was absolutely true for Brother Shields. Robbie Shields had the faith and the testimony to keep him true whether he heard the Lord's voice or not. The Lord gave him the answer to the question he had as a Sunday School teacher. I heard Brother Shields give that testimony many times.

It taught me a number of lessons in my young life. One is that the Lord does speak to us. Sometimes He speaks to us in the way that He spoke to Robbie Shields. More often than not He speaks to us in the way He spoke to Enos; that is, He speaks to our mind and to our heart, but He does speak to us. It taught me another lesson in my young life, that He doesn't usually speak to us in the classroom. I know He can speak to us any place He wishes, but usually He doesn't speak to us in the class-room, if I can say that and be understood. He doesn't always immediately speak to us when we contemplate and study and look at a question. Maybe that is a part of the preparation. I think of the Prophet Joseph Smith, who was so deeply touched by the passage in James, chapter 1, verse 5. Yet the Restoration didn't start then. The Restoration began when Joseph was in the grove, when he was on his knees, and when the Father and the Son appeared to him.

The Lord didn't speak to Robbie Shields in the classroom. He spoke to him as he was out in the world performing his everyday duties, carrying on his individual activities, doing that which was expected of him, earning his living, keeping the command-ments. I have come to know that, if the Lord is going to speak to us, that is quite often how it happens.

The Sanhedrin took great delight in counseling together and rejecting the simple and plain principles and teachings of Jesus Christ. They sat together and theorized; they discussed how wrong they thought the teachings of the Savior were. Although their own scriptures predicted that He would come, they rejected Him because they stood with their traditions rather than with the word of God. This is the reason the Savior finally said to them and to His followers, "If any man will do his will [that is, if any man will actually go out and apply these princi-ples], he shall know of the doctrine, whether it be of God, or whether I speak of myself" (John 7:17).

On another occasion He said, "By their fruits ye shall know them" (Matthew 7:20); that is, if any man will do the will of the Father, he will know that the fruit of the true gospel is good. And then He went on to talk about the person who built his foundation on the firm, hard ground as compared to the person who built his house on the sand. When the winds of adversity and change came, they blew away the house built on sand while the house built on the foundation of rock stood steady. The person who builds his faith by the process of living the com-mandments and building his testimony is on firm ground. The person who finds himself out in the field doing his duty is usually better off than the person who stands and theorizes and debates what is right and what is wrong.

And so it is with us.

The Lord usually speaks to us out in the field when we're about our business and when we're about our Father's business. Not much revelation will come until we've applied the things that we've been taught in our lives.

I'd like to tell you another story about my growing up in Tooele. When my father was stake president he called Bevan Anderson, a young stalwart in the town and a faithful soul, as a bishop. Shortly after he was called, my father had the overwhelming feeling that he should release him. He couldn't understand this because one doesn't normally call bishops and then suddenly release them. But he had this strong feeling that Bishop Anderson should be released, even though he was worthy, strong, and faithful.

My father fought this feeling; he didn't want to release him. As time went on, finally, Bevan Anderson came to him and said, "For some reason, I feel I should be released." He was soon released as bishop.

Called to take his place was O. T. Barrus. You've got to understand a little about Bishop Barrus's background. Going way back, he had a heritage of faithfulness in the Church. But in recent years Brother Barrus had not been as active in the Church as he should have been. He was a good man; but the world had gotten in the way a little bit, and he wasn't active. The Barruses had a son by the name of Dean. Dean was one of those persons who was all-everything. In everything he did, he was outstanding. He wasn't cocky or proud. He was a humble, nice person whom everybody loved. He played basketball well, he played football well, he was governor at Boys' State. In everything he touched he was a leader. He was one of those special souls the Lord sends from heaven every once in a while.

About this same time World War II broke out and young Dean Barrus found himself in navy duty. As fate would have it, the ship he was on was sunk by a submarine and his life was taken. My father told of a very sacred and personal experience after the release of Bishop Anderson. He said, "I was given to

know that in the heavens young Dean Barrus, because his life
was taken so early, was given the opportunity to have a desire
fulfilled he had for his family. It was Dean Barrus's desire that
his father might be called as a bishop, and through this action he
might be drawn into Church activity and be put in a position
where he could use his talents to serve other people in the kingdom.'' So it was, without anybody's being able to explain it,
Bevan Anderson was released with a good feeling and the realization that it was what the Lord wanted. O. T. Barrus was called
as bishop and later as stake president—a strong and faithful
member of the Church and a person who did much good before
the Lord called him home.

This sequence of events taught me some very significant lessons about a person's call and a person's release. It also taught
me something as a priesthood leader, because there have been
occasions in my own leadership duties when I have felt that
someone probably should be released. You see, a release is as
providential as a call—a release is not a punishment. We serve
because we're called, and we're released because we're called. I
have on occasion felt the inspiration of the Spirit indicating that
someone should be released at a particular time. I have fought it
on the basis that I couldn't find any outward justification for it.
I've said to myself, ''Well, I can't recommend that to the brethren around me, because I can't justify it.'' And then this experience has returned to my mind, and I've come to realize that I
indeed have a responsibility to pass it on to those of my brethren
who would make the final decision and who have the broader
light or understanding. Who knows under what circumstances a
person might be released or a person might be called? Who
knows the extent of the meaning of a man's release or a man's
call?

My father used to hire a certain carpenter. He was a very fine
man, a very sharp and astute individual. He collected quota-
tions. I still have two or three of the books that he pulled
together on the sayings of the Brethren on different subjects. He
was a tremendous gospel scholar. This man not only served a
good mission but also had gained a tremendous ability in gospel
scholarship. He knew the scriptures; he knew the gospel. However, he would go to Sunday School class and priesthood class

and disrupt everything because he was constantly correcting the teachers on little issues or bringing up dimensions of which the teachers were not aware. When he would get in a sort of cross fire with the teachers, he would usually win. This was not only frustrating to the teachers, it was disruptive to the class.

This friend of ours suddenly changed his ways. In explanation he said, "I suppose you could say that I had a revelation. For one thing, I heard heavenly choirs. Never in my entire life had I heard music like that. Oh, how I want to be there! It was a beautiful experience." Then he said, "Someone talked to me and scolded me. I was told that I must not disrupt the Sunday School and priesthood classes. 'You must not do it because you bring contention and that brings the spirit of the devil. You must not do it.' " So our friend became cooperative and helpful in his classes from that time forward.

The lesson I learned from that is that a man who uses his knowledge of the gospel of Jesus Christ to contend and to demonstrate that he knows a bit more than someone else, a man who feeds controversy by virtue of his background or his understanding of an issue, is a man who will introduce the spirit of the adversary into a gathering where the Spirit of the Lord is expected to be. It not only damages him, but it damages the faith and the testimony of the people around him long, long after the issues are forgotten. I have a feeling that long after the issues and differences of opinions have been forgotten, we will be judged by how well we upheld the priesthood and how faithful we were at bringing harmony and the Spirit of the Lord into the meetings and classes that involved us. Controversy in the Church setting invites the adversary, and this diminishes the spirit of light and truth.

Over the years I have remembered the experience of the carpenter and I have seen that upholding the priesthood is greater, far greater, in working out our own individual salvation than any controversy that we could raise to cause contention. Those kinds of things cause the influence of the adversary to affect a person's heart, and they are not according to the Lord's will. It is better that we keep the spirit of controversy out of our discussions than to feel that we are enlightening people when, in reality, all we are doing is destroying the faith and testimony of others less sure in the gospel. In the final analysis our ability to be a peacemaker and to be loyal to the priesthood might be the basic issues upon which we earn our salvation. It might be that they are far more important than the little nitty-gritty issues and tenets that come and go and will eventually be forgotten.

I would like to finish by reading from Isaiah, chapter 54, which is about the last days, about Zion, and about stakes. It is comparable to chapter 22 of 3 Nephi. It says, "No weapon that is formed against thee shall prosper." I like to think that it is directed not only to the Church, but to individual Church members who keep the faith, build their testimonies, and live by the commandments the Lord has given them, who in every sense of the word take upon them the name of Christ. Although we take his name upon us at baptism, the reality of it doesn't come until we begin to understand whether our everyday lives are in harmony with that covenant. "No weapon that is formed against thee shall prosper; and every tongue that shall rise against thee in judgment thou shalt condemn. This is the heritage of the servants of the Lord, and their righteousness is of me, saith the Lord." (Isaiah 54:17; see also 3 Nephi 22:17.)

Now, I've talked today about my heritage and about the heritage of my community. For that heritage I am humbly grateful. I boast of nothing myself. Anything that I might be able to contribute to my position or my life has been given to me by those who made the sacrifice before I even came to mortality. I am grateful to them; and I am grateful for the gospel of Jesus Christ, that offers me the promise of standing before a father and a grandfather again, embracing them as family members united in this great cause.

I suppose one final gift which I received by way of heritage—because I can't remember when it came into my life—was the spirit and blessing of testimony. The faith and prayers evidenced in our household caused me to recognize the truthfulness of gospel principles from my very earliest recollections. I felt it was true a long time before I understood it, and I knew it was true before I knew entirely what it was that was true. So great was the faith and testimony in our household that our allegiance to the gospel was total.

My heritage is not so different from your heritage, because when we embrace the gospel of Jesus Christ, we have a common heritage. It is a doctrinal and spiritual heritage, and what is shared by one is shared by all. We are all a party to the Father and the Son's appearing to the Prophet Joseph Smith. We are all a party to Brigham Young's standing and supporting and sustaining the Prophet Joseph Smith through some terribly difficult times. We are all a party to the spiritual heritage of the gospel and the blessings that are promised to those who believe in the kingdom of God.

Has all of this stopped since Joseph Smith and Brigham Young and Wilford Woodruff? I submit to you that these blessings are here today in their fulness, and I say to you that the Lord speaks to you and me. The fact that he speaks is not unusual, but it does little good unless we are listening, unless we reach back into our common heritage, unless we keep the commandments. The promptings of the Holy Spirit need to become a part of our lives so that we are willing to accept them, be inspired by them, and live by them.

This is our common heritage. May the Lord bless us that no controversy, no doctrine as taught by the principles of men (see 2 Nephi 28:31), no personal disagreement, no unrepented sin will become so big and so powerful that it will take away from us our spiritual heritage. May our spiritual heritage last long after issues are forgotten and men are dead. May the Lord bless us to this end.

I bear you my witness that the work is true. I testify to you that I know that God lives. I know He lives; I know that Jesus is the Christ, the Savior of the World, the Author of this work. I know that Joseph Smith saw what he said he saw. I know that our Church President is a prophet of God today. This is the gospel of Jesus Christ; this is His holy work; this is His way. May the Lord bless us that we may honor our heritage and stand firm for that which is true.

Make Summer Count

Our ability to reach out to others and to render real service is one of the most divine things we can do. We serve others best when our lives reflect that which we would like to bring into the lives of others, so that our words and actions combine to help point out a better way.

I have had several young people say to me, "I want to do something meaningful this summer; I want to participate in some cause. I want to help the needy if I can."

I would like to suggest some guidelines that might be helpful for you to follow as you strive to help other people or become involved in worthy community projects. We live in a day and age when more and more people are interested in helping their fellowmen. Many young people are involved in this kind of service, and this is to your credit.

Let me read a few verses from the Doctrine and Covenants about helping the needy. The Lord, speaking to the Prophet Joseph, says, "Wo unto you rich men, that will not give your substance to the poor, for your riches will canker your souls; and this shall be your lamentation in the day of visitation, and of judgment, and of indignation: The harvest is past, the summer is ended, and my soul is not saved!" (D&C 56:16.)

So the Lord has a few words for the person who is in a position to help and does not help. Then he goes further and makes a statement that I think is interesting: "Wo unto you poor men,

---

Devotional address given at Brigham Young University May 1971.

whose hearts are not broken, whose spirits are not contrite, and whose bellies are not satisfied, and whose hands are not stayed from laying hold upon other men's goods, whose eyes are full of greediness, and who will not labor with your own hands!'' (D&C 56:17.)

So he has a word too for those who might be the recipients of aid. Then he goes on to say, "But blessed are the poor who are pure in heart, whose hearts are broken, and whose spirits are contrite, for they shall see the kingdom of God" (D&C 56:18).

We must agree that we cannot do all things for all people; and since we cannot help everyone who really needs it, perhaps the best place to start is with those projects and people where our contribution can make the greatest difference. Some militants that we hear so much about fall into the category of men whose hearts are not broken, whose spirits are not contrite, and who are not satisfied with what they receive. I am sure that these people need help as well as everyone else. If, however, we have to start someplace, and we want our contribution to be meaningful, maybe the best place to start is with those people who are of such a mind and attitude that they will not only receive the contribution but will also find it helpful and useful.

Maybe I am speaking a little pessimistically, but as I have looked over many large programs—both governmental and private—I think we must conclude that many of these programs have produced minimal results. Money can, should, and does play a part in many of these programs; yet it is becoming obvious that money alone will not solve the problems of the needy. It will not cause the problems of the needy to go away. Funding is not the sole answer to the problems that face us.

As far as money itself is concerned, I am reminded of a story that made the rounds a few years ago about the vagrant who went into the Office of Economic Opportunity in Washington. He was looking for a dime for a cup of coffee. He came out with a Community Action Grant for $175,000, three staff assistants, and six VISTA volunteers. Again, it appears that money alone is not the answer.

I would like to suggest some guidelines whereby members of

the Church might effectively participate in and contribute to helping other people. I believe that we should ask ourselves four basic questions to guide us.

Question number one is, Am I helping, or am I part of the problem? Sometimes the people who are the most eager to help turn out to be the people with the problems. As individuals in this society and this Church, we must look to ourselves and say: "Do I have any serious problems that I must work out first? Is there any serious repentance that I must take care of before I go out and try to help someone else? What must I do for myself so that when I come to these people I can come as an example, and not suffer from problems that would prevent me from giving the most dedicated and effective service I can?"

The Savior made this very point when He said, "Physician, heal thyself" (Luke 4:23). On another occasion He said, "And if the blind lead the blind, both shall fall into the ditch" (Matthew 15:14). So the first question is, In what condition am I?

Question number two should be, Is my family in need of help? Should I be helping others if my own family is in need? Could my contribution be in their direction? Sometimes this becomes difficult because the closer we are to people, the harder it is to help them. But certainly if our family and loved ones are in need of assistance or help, we should do what we can for them before we go out and try to help others.

Question number three is, Does someone need help in my ward or branch? I honestly believe that the Lord and society expect us to take care of our own members before we go out into the world. Can you imagine what this world would be like if we started with the premise that every church should take care of its own members—honestly aid and assist them to meet their problems, get back on their feet, and help them where necessary? We would go a long way toward the solution of some of our most critical problems. As Latter-day Saints, we should first look to the needs of members of our own Church before we go to the world.

I would suggest that when you go home this summer, you contact your bishop or branch president. Find out if there is anything you can do. Somebody in your own ward, in your own branch, may be in need. Find out if there is some project that you can become involved in.

Question number four concerns the rest of our world: Finally, after we have looked at ourselves, at our own families, at the members of the Church, are there worthy projects in our neighborhood, community, city, or even at the national and international level that we should concern ourselves with? We do our best work, however, when we start with ourselves and progress outward.

I know of a young father who lives in a large city. He was very concerned because he found that his daughter was tampering with drugs. There was not much communication between the father and the daughter, so he did what he could to understand her better. He even began to associate with the young people involved in the drug scene. He began to go to the areas where drugs changed hands, and he became quite a popular figure among some of these people.

One thing led to another. Finally, he had convinced himself that in order to understand these young people and their problems, he would have to experience what they experienced. I am not in favor of that reasoning. Some people say, "Well, if you have never experienced it, how do you know?" I think that Art Linkletter's answer is best: "Neither have the world's best baby doctors had any babies."

This father became so involved that he began to neglect and forget his family. Experimentation with drugs led to immorality. Today this man is popular with some young people who have drug problems. The tragedy is that he has the same problems they do—and worse. He is now separated from his wife; his children are on the verge of juvenile delinquency; there is sorrow in the home. His daughter came in to see me one day. She said, "Oh, if only Dad would tell me not to do the things I do, but he is so involved himself that all he can say is, 'Well, make up your own mind.' Isn't that a tragedy? I don't have a father anymore." A case of the blind trying to lead the blind.

The Lord and our society expect us to take care of ourselves first—that is, to make sure that we are free from serious problems; second, to help our families in case there are problems at that level; and third, to aid the members of our own Church. Then let's move from that point into the programs and activities that will allow us to make the best kind of contribution to our community and the world.

While I consider myself no expert in the field of projects for the needy, I have made observations about some programs that I have been involved in during the past few years. It appears that most successful programs for helping people have three or four important characteristics. We could look for these when we are searching for a program in which to become involved.

The first characteristic is that the program, for the most part, involves or is run by volunteer help. There is something pure about a person's coming to help someone else because he really wants to do it and not because someone has paid him.

The second major characteristic is that the most successful projects deal with education, training, or learning. There are many projects and activities today that deal with symptoms, not causes. The best projects are those that help train, retrain, or educate people, who can then compete and—with the help of their own dignity and self-esteem—work themselves out of their problems. Perhaps they cannot do this alone, but at least they are lifted to a level where they can be more effective and responsible. These educational, training, and learning projects are the kinds that deal with the problems and not just the symptoms. They are involved in building and not tearing down.

Another vital characteristic is the kind of attention many projects are given. Some of the most effective work done in this country is carried on in a very quiet, unpretentious way by people who are not too concerned about whether they get attention for what they do. There is nothing belligerent or rebellious about their work. I think of the Savior's advice when He said (and I am paraphrasing, of course), "Do this kind of work in private, and the Lord—seeing that you have done it in private—will reward you openly." (See Matthew 6:3–4.) There is something admirable about an unpretentious volunteer effort to help somebody in a cause that may not receive any publicity but nonetheless is effective and right.

Not many years ago, while I was living in New York City, I was employed by the Fresh Air Fund. I was impressed by this organization because a handful of paid employees organize a program that collects millions of dollars every year and uses it to send needy children from New York City to volunteer families in surrounding states. The fund is one of the oldest philanthropic endeavors in the United States. It was organized back before the turn of the century when children were literally starving to death. They needed to be fed, and they needed health care. Now that private and government organizations have met most of those needs, the fund has turned to yet another very useful and effective endeavor. The children now come out every summer for what they call "friendly town vacations." They go to volunteer families. The money collected is to help screen the children, make sure that their health is all right, and then provide their transportation. All the rest is volunteer.

Most of the children who go into these homes do not have a father; some of them do not have a mother. And in this society the best way a person can know how to be a good father or a good mother, or a good husband or a good wife, is by what he sees in his own home. Most practical training we get is from the experiences we go through as we are growing up. We decide what we want to do, and perhaps what we do not want to do, on the basis of what we have seen in our home. How can a young man show his role and responsibility as a father if there has never been a father image in his life to show him? Thus the fund will place a child with a family where he can see what a father does and what a mother does, how young people and children react in a family situation.

The program has been eminently successful because the young people return home realizing that the words *father, mother,* and *family* can really mean something. The experience extends their horizons. They tend to stay in school longer because they can see that there is something more for them if they will prepare themselves. It helps to influence their lives. One of the Fresh Air Fund graduates was Charles Wilson, the former chairman of the board of General Motors. And believe it or not, Danny Kaye is a product of the Fresh Air Fund program —and there have been many others.

In closing, I want to enlist you in a program. It is a volunteer program wherein you can make a contribution that will be real and far reaching. For instance, the volunteers who participated in this program last year alone changed the lives of hundreds of thousands of people throughout the world. I do not know of a single program or combination of programs that has reached so many people, turned them in a direction that is both beneficial and good, brought more happiness and stronger family ties, and provided greater blessings and peace of mind. The program is not just temporary; it does not end after these volunteers leave. What it gives is permanent. Now that has to be some kind of program, and it is!

Maybe you have guessed by now that I am talking about the missionary program. Thousands of souls were converted last year. You show me a single program that begins to even approximate that result. What I would like you to do is to go home now and become part of that volunteer force. Find a family this summer, will you? Take them the gospel of Jesus Christ. There are many returned missionaries in this audience, and they know what I am talking about. You will never have a better experience in your life. You will never have a greater experience of giving, of meaningful activity, and of seeing an actual and literal positive change come into the life of an individual.

This can be the best possible way for a person to make a contribution. You may ask, "How do I go about it?" Well, the specifics are these. When you get home or to wherever you are going, contact your bishop or your branch president and ask him to put you in touch with the ward or branch mission leader. This individual will suggest to you how to get started.

Missionary work will not take your whole summer or all of your time. But if you are successful as part of this great army of volunteers, you will have made a contribution this summer that will far exceed anything that you could have possibly done otherwise. I am not saying that you should not participate in other projects. I am recommending to you a program that really, honestly, sincerely makes a difference. As an example, let me share with you a letter. It was written a few months ago by someone with a friend who thought enough of him to do exactly what we have been talking about. That is, the writer is a convert to the Church. He had a friend who brought him the gospel of Jesus Christ.

A few years ago, after this person became a member of the Church and received the priesthood, he was married for time and eternity. A few months ago a terrible tragedy struck. His wife died suddenly; there was no warning. Here was this man with a little girl and no wife. This is the letter he wrote while in the depths of his sorrow:

> I am so miserable and lonely. I loved her so much, and the separation is so painful. I know the gospel is true. I know she is alive and working on her new assignment, but I do not find as much comfort as I thought I would.
>
> I see good in all this. I see that my character can be strengthened. I see that my testimony has increased. I am grateful that I am a Latter-day Saint. I am appreciative that I have a knowledge of the truth and that I hold the priesthood.
>
> If I did not have my testimony or my temple marriage, life would be so cumbersome. But the gospel is true, God lives, and Jesus the Christ, his Son, lives. Because he lives, she lives; and I will live. Because of my priesthood and the sealing powers of that priesthood, we will be reunited. That I know with a certainty tested in the flames of sorrow. But I miss the girl, my sweetheart. We were one, and half of me is beyond the veil.

This summer, if you can present to someone the faith and knowledge and testimony to carry them through trials such as this, you will have made one of the greatest contributions that any human being can make to another. Pray that we may go to our fellowmen and give them the water that will cause them to thirst no more. Will you not accept this challenge and make your summer meaningful?

Sacrifice

A clear message from the scriptures and the inspired teachings of living prophets is the role that sacrifice plays in the gospel of Jesus Christ. It is a divine law which, when properly applied, opens the windows of heaven, changes the nature of the Lord's children, and leads them to eternal life.

It seems one word is always mentioned in connection with the Aaronic and Melchizedek priesthoods, whenever these priesthoods are on the earth, and that word is *sacrifice*. Sacrifices were offered on altars by holders of the priesthood as recorded in the Old Testament. There are also sacrifices of a more personal nature that the Lord requires of those who have taken upon themselves the gospel of Jesus Christ.

From the very beginning the Lord required sacrifices. When Adam and Eve were driven out of the Garden of Eden, they were commanded to

> offer the firstlings of their flocks, for an offering unto the Lord. And Adam was obedient unto the commandment of the Lord.
>
> And after many days an angel of the Lord appeared unto Adam, saying: Why dost thou offer sacrifices unto the Lord? And Adam said unto him: I know not, save the Lord commanded me.
>
> And then the angel spake, saying: This thing is a similitude of the sacrifice of the Only Begotten of the Father, which is full of grace and truth.
>
> Wherefore, thou shalt do all that thou doest in the name of the Son, and thou shalt repent and call upon God in the name of the Son forevermore. (Moses 5:5–8.)

Address given at Australia and New Zealand area conferences December 1979.

Thus, sacrifice as a means of directing man's attention to the sacrifice of the Son of God was part of the true form of worship from the very beginning.

Elder Bruce R. McConkie has written: "The chief and most important symbolism in all the feasts [of ancient Israel] was that shown forth through the sacrificial ordinances. These bore record of the coming sacrifice of the Lamb of God and taught the people how redemption came and how sins were to be remitted by the sprinkling of his blood." (*The Mortal Messiah: From Bethlehem to Calvary* [Salt Lake City: Deseret Book Company, 1979], 1:178.)

With the death, burial, and resurrection of Christ, the offering of sacrifices was done away with and was replaced by the sacrament. Said the resurrected Lord to the Nephites: "And ye shall offer up unto me no more the shedding of blood; yea, your sacrifices and your burnt offerings shall be done away, for I will accept none of your sacrifices and burnt offerings. And ye shall offer for a sacrifice unto me a broken heart and a contrite spirit." (3 Nephi 9:19–20.)

The offering of these sacrifices after the time of Moses and up to the time of Christ was the responsibility of the Aaronic Priesthood, just as the administration and passing of the sacrament is the responsibility of the Aaronic Priesthood today. The sacrament today draws the mind of the true worshipper to the Savior and his great atoning sacrifice. It also is designed so that we can renew our covenants and seek an outpouring of the Spirit, the same objectives of the true sacrificial ceremonies offered by ancient Israel.

Having briefly talked about ancient sacrifices, I would now like to talk about the principle of sacrifice.

President N. Eldon Tanner defined sacrifice as "going without or giving up something which is good for something which is better." From the Church point of view, the law of sacrifice is an extremely important part of the gospel and absolutely essential in order to gain eternal life. Because all things belong to the Lord, those who truly love Him should be willing to return to Him whatever is required of them. The sacrifice the Lord requires of us, if it can be called such, is the willingness to give up earthly things for the sake of receiving the greatest of all gifts—eternal life.

There is another important reason for the principle and law of sacrifice: sacrifice develops faith, and faith is the foundation stone in the Lord's plan for the exaltation of His children. Joseph Smith taught the following:

> A religion that does not require the sacrifice of all things never has power sufficient to produce the faith necessary unto life and salvation. . . . It was through this sacrifice, and this only, that God has ordained that men should enjoy eternal life; and it is through the medium of the sacrifice of all earthly things that men do actually know that they are doing the things that are well pleasing in the sight of God. When a man has offered in sacrifice all that he has for the truth's sake, . . . believing before God that he has been called to make this sacrifice because he seeks to do his will, he does know, most assuredly, that God does and will accept his sacrifice and offering, and that he has not, nor will not seek his face in vain. Under these circumstances, then, he can obtain the faith necessary for him to lay hold on eternal life. . . .
>
> Those, then, who make the sacrifice, will have the testimony that their course is pleasing in the sight of God; and those who have this testimony will have faith to lay hold on eternal life, and will be enabled, through faith, to endure unto the end, and receive the crown that is laid up for them that love the appearing of our Lord Jesus Christ. But those who do not make the sacrifice cannot enjoy this faith, because men are dependent upon this sacrifice in order to obtain this faith: therefore, they cannot lay hold upon eternal life. (*Lectures on Faith* [Salt Lake City: Bookcraft, n.d.], 6:7, 10.)

Sacrifice in today's Church does not usually mean giving one's life (although some have had to do it in the past) or giving up all we possess. Few of us are called on to give up much of what we possess. What we must be willing to do is to sacrifice whatever is required of us, whether it be time, talents, riches, the praise and honor of men, or anything else we may have to offer, to the extent the Lord may require it. We must be prepared to do whatever might be required; if we are willing, then the sacrifice is acceptable, even though it may never actually be required of us.

The Lord requires a willing heart and mind (see D&C 64:34; 97:8). As members of the Lord's Church and as priesthood holders, we are fortunate to have a heritage of sacrifice to show us the way. The great faith of our pioneer ancestors was forged by the sacrifices they made in order to establish the gospel of Jesus Christ in these last days. These sacrifices are the heritage of every man, woman, and child in the Church. For instance, take the winter of 1846 and 1847. Having been driven out of Nauvoo, the city they had built and made beautiful, the Saints established a temporary settlement on the Missouri River. Their plan was to prepare through the winter for an exodus the following spring into the unknown west.

The settlement took on the appearance of an established community that winter; even schools for the children were successfully started. But this was not without its sacrifice, for nearly six hundred Saints lost their lives in that place, many of them children. One account states: "Often a pupil—sometimes several—did not appear when the school bell rang. A type of scurvy, called black canker, took a sorrowful toll. Lack of proper nourishment, insufficient shelter, extremes of temperature in the lowlands along the river—made the people easy victims of disease." (Gordon B. Hinckley, *Truth Restored* [Salt Lake City: Deseret News Press, 1947], p. 101.)

Today, in the old cemetery of that encampment, there is a heroic monument. It depicts a mother and father laying a child in a grave, a grave they knew they would never again visit as they made their way west with the rest of the pioneers. The name of the settlement—Winter Quarters.

It has been said that sacrifice is also the deepest and purest expression of love. If we love the Lord with all our hearts, it is easier to sacrifice the things necessary to keep His commandments.

I had a close friend who discovered the blessings associated with sacrifice when he was seventeen years of age. My friend was on the local football team in the city where he lived. The coach of that team was his idol, and he took every opportunity to be with that coach and learn from him.

During football's off-season, the coach had a job as a lifeguard at the local swimming pool. During the summer the coach wanted to get away for a two-week holiday. He looked around for someone to fill in for him, but could find no one. He finally turned to my friend one day and said, "You have taken a course in lifesaving. Why don't you fill in for the two weeks and I will pay you?''

Despite knowing that he would be by himself and being frightened at the responsibility, he nevertheless said yes; he didn't want his coach to think he couldn't do anything that his coach thought he could do.

As the day came for the coach to leave, my friend's nervousness increased until he finally did something he had never done before. Going on the faith he had in the Lord, he turned to Him in prayer and promised the Lord that out of the earnings of those two weeks he would return to the Lord not just a tenth (which was, of course, his tithing), but he would divide the whole amount and return half to the Lord—if the Lord would provide that no serious problem arose during those two weeks and my friend would have the ability to do what was expected of him.

My friend had plans for that money, so giving up half of it was no small sacrifice. But after having made the promise, he had a very interesting experience. As the day came for him to start, a confidence and peace came into his heart, and he knew with a certainty that everything would go well. It was a confidence greater than anything he had experienced in his young life. Everything went well for the entire two weeks. At the end of this time he completed his agreement with the Lord by contributing half of what he received. Looking back on the experience, my friend said: ''I can't tell you how much faith and confidence that gave me in the Lord. While I have never felt the need to repeat that kind of experience, I have always been willing and even happy to pay my tithing. I have discovered for myself that a willingness to sacrifice a few temporal things and comply with the laws of God really does bring forth the blessings of heaven.''

What might be some specific sacrifices required of priesthood holders today, sacrifices necessary to develop faith and love of God that will lead to eternal life? Let me list a few and divide them in two categories: Melchizedek Priesthood holders and Aaronic Priesthood holders.

Under Melchizedek Priesthood I would list the following:

1. Sacrifice everything necessary so you can be eligible to go to the temple. It is here that the true meaning of sacrifice is taught.

2. Sacrifice the worldly feelings of selfishness and lack of faith that may prevent you from paying a full tithe. This will nourish your faith, increase your spirituality, and open the door for temporal blessings.

3. Sacrifice all immoral thoughts and actions so your marriage will be pure and your family strong.

4. Sacrifice the passiveness and fear of men that might prevent you from bringing a family into the Church.

5. Sacrifice all negative comments and behavior. A Melchizedek Priesthood holder is a believer, a man of faith. In priesthood councils, in Church classes and meetings, and in his home, he must build the faith of others by being an example of the believer, by faithful conversation, and by constantly building and lifting. Always be the one to be counted on for enlightenment, vision, and encouragement.

6. Sacrifice the old ways of doing things if they don't meet with modern revelation and current priesthood procedure. In all things follow the living prophets. The person who went before you may not have done it entirely right. Look to the scriptures. Look to the priesthood.

7. Sacrifice whatever is necessary to teach the gospel to your family in your home. Use all the Church resources necessary, but do not, as a Melchizedek Priesthood holder, let go of your spiritual responsibilities to your family.

8. Sacrifice any disloyalties. Stand with your priesthood leaders and uphold them in public and private and the Lord will uphold you.

And now to the youth of the Aaronic Priesthood:

1. Sacrifice any feelings of disloyalty. Uphold the gospel of Jesus Christ wherever you are. Uphold the Church and your priesthood leaders. Uphold your country. If you do these things, the Lord will uphold you.

2. Sacrifice all things that will prevent you from preparing to serve the Savior in the mission field when you reach the proper age.

3. Sacrifice all the worldly things that will keep you from a temple marriage at the right time. You will have more happiness and greater opportunities for success by doing it the Lord's way.

4. Sacrifice all feelings that would prevent you from honoring your father and your mother. Your Heavenly Father and

mother love a person who shows respect for his earthly father and mother.

5. Sacrifice all the worldly influences that might prevent you from going to the Lord and receiving a convincing testimony that Jesus is the Christ and that this church is true.

6. Sacrifice the occasional feelings that you have to follow or be like those around you who don't know the purpose of life. The Lord conferred on you the priesthood so you could show others the light. He did not intend for you to get lost with them in the darkness.

7. Sacrifice everything that might mislead the world as to who you really are and what you really stand for.

8. Sacrifice your feelings of inferiority and lack of self-worth. The very fact that you are a child of God and have the gospel makes you a person of great worth before the Lord and a great servant to your fellowmen.

9. Sacrifice the feelings of not wanting to achieve. The Lord wants you to be the best of whatever you find yourself fitted to be. Prayerfully work at it until you are the best, no matter what it is.

10. Sacrifice any feelings of selfishness. Your priesthood has been conferred on you so you can serve your fellowmen. Work at helping others.

11. Sacrifice the time and effort necessary to graduate from seminary and institute. This will help secure your knowledge and faith in the gospel.

Brethren, these are the kinds of sacrifices the Lord requires of us today. At this time and throughout our lives, may we offer an offering unto the Lord in righteousness. May we gladly offer up all that is required.

May both the law and spirit of sacrifice to the Lord govern our lives, all to the honor and glory of His holy name.

IV.
Seeking
The Truth

To those who have tasted the water at many wells only to
find that the unquenching thirst of the soul
drives them on in search of that which will bring peace
and nourishment to the heart . . . , will you not come
and drink from this well, . . . and see if you
have not found the waters of life where you can drink
and thirst no more?

Receiving a Prophet

Our search for truth must sooner or later involve whom we decide to follow. The world has its heroes and many of these have something good to offer. Yet to have the opportunity to follow someone who has been actually called of God and is divinely inspired exceeds any experience the world has to offer.

I want to begin by bearing testimony to you of the truthfulness of this work. I know that God lives and that Jesus is the Christ; this is their work. I know that Joseph Smith was a prophet of God, and that we have a living prophet of God today.

I would like to share an experience or two with you. When I was growing up, Heber J. Grant was the President of the Church. My father always prayed for President Grant. He had great personal feeling for him because President Grant at one time had been president of the Tooele Stake, and my father at that time was now president of the Tooele Stake. When I was a young boy, President Grant became ill and passed away. I can remember after the funeral kneeling in family prayer and hearing my father praying with the same love and devotion and feeling for the next President of the Church, George Albert Smith.

As a youth, I was surprised because I had never heard anybody pray for any prophet other than Heber J. Grant. And I felt almost cheated—like my father was turning away from a good friend. But as the time went on, through that experience and other experiences, he taught me a very valuable lesson—you

Address given at general conference April 1983.

see, he had great love and appreciation for President Grant, and that would never change; but in his heart I realized that he had saved his greatest love and his greatest loyalty for his God, and whomever God would send he would sustain and uphold and pray for and embrace.

Not very long ago, I had the opportunity to preside over the Australia Sydney Mission. I had come out of the Missionary Department, and I suppose my missionary views were very conservative. At any rate, as we began our work in the Australia Sydney Mission, we had some modest, but good, successes, and I felt comfortable about what we were doing—until President Kimball spoke to us. In his own manner and in his own way, he said, "Brother Dunn, Loren, we must all lengthen our stride." And I got the message.

The message was that although we had made progress, before the Lord and before the prophet, it wasn't enough. We went back and redoubled our efforts; we found increased growth, but we also found increased strength, and new stakes evolved because of those efforts. I don't think the progress was so much because of us, but because of our desire to follow the prophet.

I was talking to a priesthood leader just last weekend. We had finished our Saturday night leadership meeting, which was on missionary work, and he said to me, "You know, you are really a missionary General Authority." And I said, "No, I don't consider myself a missionary General Authority. If I can be remembered for anything (and I hope that somehow, somewhere I can), I would settle for that which my father taught me and for which I feel he was known, and that is one who is willing to give allegiance to and follow a prophet of God. And if that can be my lot, then I feel I will have accomplished the thing the Lord has sent me to do."

It's not the program, it's not the activities, but in the final analysis it is our loyalty to him whom God has called and the offering of our prayers on his behalf.

There is a scripture that goes this way: "He that receiveth a prophet in the name of a prophet shall receive a prophet's reward" (Matthew 10:41). I have come to realize the literalness of that promise. I've seen those blessings in the life of my father because of his loyalty. I would like those blessings for my family and myself, and I would like to see those blessings in the life of every Latter-day Saint.

May I end where I began. God does live, Jesus is the Christ. Joseph Smith is a true prophet, and we are led by a prophet of God today. The prophet has my loyalty and he has my love, because how can I uphold the Lord unless I uphold him?

Communication, Truth, and Knowledge

At best, communication is an imperfect process. What we understand from what others say to us is based on the meaning we give to their words and on our experiences. But communication becomes more accurate and precise when the influence of the Holy Ghost is added. It touches hearts with meaning and understanding and brings unity.

Perhaps you remember reading in the papers about a hearing in Washington, D.C., to investigate an oil seepage problem off the West Coast of the United States. A reporter for one of the prominent newspapers in this country excused himself from the hearing, and, as they do many times, he asked the reporter next to him to keep track of the proceedings. He came back a few minutes later and reviewed the summary of testimony made by his associate. The man testifying was the head of a large oil company, and the summary the reporter read indicated that this man had said he was not concerned about conservation or about how people could get excited about the death of a few birds.

This, of course, was reported immediately and appeared on the front page of many of the papers in the United States. It turned out later that this report was wrong, and when the news media found what the facts were, they printed retractions trying to correct the situation. I think this incident indicates to us that we live in a very complex society. The need to know has never been greater, yet our communication processes do not always meet the challenge. We may obtain a great deal of information,

Devotional address given at Brigham Young University April 1969.

but it is hard to say how accurate this information is. And as time goes on, it becomes more difficult for us to determine what is true and what is not true.

This is the communication process. People say words to us, and we say words to them; but understanding comes when we look to our own experiences and try to attach meaning to the words that are said to us. If the person who is talking to us has not had the same experiences we have had, then perhaps we will attach different meaning to the words he is using. So you see, the process of communication is, at best, an inaccurate tool and is subject to breakdown. Nonetheless, as humans, we have been remarkably successful in our communication. Still we must be careful today, possibly more than ever before, that we are not misled, and that we gather as much good information as possible so that our value judgments may be as accurate and effective as possible.

Let's move into the university area for just a moment. A few years ago I was a guest lecturer at Boston University. I can't think of anything more stimulating than to try to keep up with a group of university students from day to day; it's a great experience. But there seems to be something happening in our universities which I am not sure is good. The learning process is getting all tangled up with the personal opinions and prejudices of those who teach.

I think in some respects (it's true at least at some institutions) the university professor is interpreting for the class rather than presenting to the class as much of the overall picture as he possibly can. I've seen this in the area of philosophy, where an instructor will interpret for the class that which he feels is right, perhaps even insisting that it is right. Such insistence is in itself a violation of the true academic approach. When we sit in a classroom, we have a right to know at least as many sides of a particular issue as we can possibly hear, and no professor has the right to expound his own approach in a public school to the exclusion of other points of view.

This is a vital part of the communication process, because without it a person may go out of the classroom believing there is only one point of view with regard to a particular social situation. We need to get the whole picture, and our professors and instructors need to realize that they have a sacred obligation to present the entire picture.

I bring this to your minds hoping that as you go forward in your own lives you will remember that the need to know has never been greater. But you must be careful of those who would mislead you.

Another aspect of the need to know is the generation gap. My grandparents come over from Kirkintilloch, Scotland, and settled in Tooele. At the tender age of sixty Grandfather started a newspaper, and when he got to be about eighty years old my father began to help him in the business. Because Grandfather had particular ideas as to how things should be run, there were differences of opinion. My father was trying to introduce new machinery and new innovations into the business, but Grandfather just couldn't see it. This led to some rather interesting discussions, as only it can between Scotchmen. I didn't know my grandfather, but my father tells of having a particularly stimulating discussion with him one day when Grandfather suddenly turned to him and said, "Now, son, why can ye no' be like me? Why can ye no' be agreeable?"

My father passed away about five years ago. He was a very innovative man, and he introduced some important concepts that strengthened our business and caused it to grow. But then my brother came along—the third generation—and he had still newer and more innovative ideas, some of which I don't think my father completely grasped because, you see, they were of two different generations.

Fortunately, there wasn't the difficulty between my brother and father that there was between my father and grandfather, because they understood one another better.

My brother now heads the business, and he has introduced the computer and other innovations. But I suspect that in a few years hence, one of his boys will come up and say, "Now, Dad, there is a better way, and there is an easier way"; and I suspect that if Dad is like the rest of us, he will say, "Now wait a minute, son." And there might be a little debate about what is good and what is bad.

I am reminded of the elderly Vermonter who was seated in his rocking chair enjoying the view from his front porch. A tourist came up to the old gentleman and said, "Well, sir, I guess you've seen a lot of changes over the years."

"Yes," replied the Vermonter, "and I've opposed every one of them!"

To me, this is the generation gap. But I do think that the younger generation, being usually more flexible, has a great responsibility to close the generation gap—perhaps even a greater responsibility than the older generation.

I suspect you can be more successful in trying to understand what the older generation is saying to you than perhaps they can in trying to understand what you mean. This modern world as it stands today, with all its innovation and advanced science and technology, would make it harder for them, I think, to come to a complete understanding of your point of view than for you to reach out and try to find meaning in what they are trying to say. Try to keep this in mind as you seek to establish communication with your elders.

Let's move from there to the need to know ourselves. A young girl came to my office the other day; she is a BYU student from California. A number of her friends had been attending school in different institutions of higher learning around the country. She had friends who were part of the entire spectrum of student life today, from the "way out" to the "way in." She made a point about some of these friends, which I thought was very well put. She said, "You know, the people who go out and buck the institutions and go against society usually have one thing in common: they have an appalling lack of respect for themselves. They seem to have no idea who they are, and they act like people who are striving and searching and yearning just to be recognized."

I can understand a person who feels that way. I may not be able to respect what he does to gain identity, but the need to be recognized in one way or another is within all people. The problem we face is that group pressures and the desire to be accepted by those around us may cause us to alter our course drastically if we are not sure of where we are going in the first place, and why.

All of us here presumably have the inner knowledge that life has an eternal purpose. We are anchored by the realization that we are literally the children of God and that he has given us a complete set of divine rules designed to bring all men back into His presence. If this inner knowledge is truly our own, our testimony, then we will be better able to face the group and individual pressures that are found in school and other walks of life—pressures that point toward immorality and physical abuse and godlessness, pressures that may be tempting because we don't know ourselves well enough to withstand the enticement of those who demonstrate their own lack of self-respect by showing no real respect for others.

The greatest need we have today as individuals is to know ourselves. To me, this means a knowledge of our relationship to God and a realization of our importance as His children. This is the knowledge that leads not to false pride but to a humble self-respect, an inner peace and strength that allows us to be ourselves in the face of adverse group and individual pressures.

May we all be able to look within ourselves and find something there we can hang on to. Let us be sure that it is strong enough and grounded well enough that storms from the outside don't alter or weaken it. We'll learn through that to respect ourselves, and we'll find more peace of mind. The need to know ourselves, then, becomes of basic importance, and this knowledge comes as we draw close to the Lord.

We have now discussed how communication is an imperfect instrument at best when it depends on imperfect man. Because of this, it is hard to know anything with complete accuracy. But now consider the type of communication in which one of the parties is a divine, perfect being, and for the first time absolute knowledge becomes possible. For the first time, ultimate truth becomes possible.

Consider this statement from scripture:

> And now, after the many testimonies which have been given of him, this is the testimony, last of all, which we give of him: That he lives!
>
> For we saw him, even on the right hand of God; and we heard the voice bearing record that he is the Only Begotten of the Father—
>
> That by him, and through him, and of him, the worlds are and were created, and the inhabitants thereof are begotten sons and daughters unto God. (D&C 76:22–24.)

This testimony expresses a perfect knowledge that cannot come just by viewing something with the eyes. When the Savior asked his disciples who He, the Savior, was, the Apostle Peter answered, "Thou art the Christ, the Son of the living God" (Matthew 16:16), to which the Savior replied, "Flesh and blood hath not revealed it unto thee, but my Father which is in heaven" (Matthew 16:17). There is, then, a way to know things as they really are which is more perfect and more accurate and more true than any mortal way, and that is to have something confirmed by the Holy Ghost. Peter denied the Savior three times prior to the Savior's crucifixion but turned out to be one of the Lord's most valiant and brave followers, with an almost perfect knowledge of His divine mission. The power and conviction which Peter had came from the gift of the Holy Ghost. This gift did things for Peter that his own physical senses could not accomplish; he saw the Savior with his eyes, but he did not have the power or the great testimony until the Holy Ghost bore witness to his soul.

So by adding one ingredient, we cause the process of communication to take on an entirely new and powerful dimension. That ingredient is the influence of the Holy Ghost, and it is capable of making clear to everyone who receives it what the truth really is. To experience the influence of this gift is to have one of the greatest experiences available to man. As leaders of the Church communicate with us, as the Lord communicates with us both personally and through the scriptures, we are urged and admonished to "seek the Spirit" so that we might know the truthfulness and importance of their message. When one has that experience, there can be no doubt as to what is right and what is wrong.

As we consider the things of man today, let us be careful and do all within our power to know as much as we can, still realizing that there are ways that we might be misled. But let us also realize that this gift of the Holy Ghost, if cultivated, can ultimately deliver to us a knowledge of the truth. It can not only help us in developing a perfect knowledge of the truths of the gospel of Jesus Christ, but it can also bring us to a knowledge of the truth of all things if we make it a part of our communication process. It will help to keep us from being deceived by the teachings and doctrines of men; and it will ultimately train our dispositions to seek out that which is important and to understand that which is true.

Do you remember the accounts of the time when Joseph Smith was translating the Book of Mormon? They suggest that at first he used the Urim and Thummim, but that after a while he had so fully developed these qualities of translation that he was able to translate without the Urim and Thummim. The gift of the Holy Ghost will do the same thing in our lives. It will temper our dispositions so that truth and light and understanding will become part of us, second nature to us, and we will know them and understand them and delight in them. This truly is a gift of God, even the Spirit that manifests the revelations of God.

How can we cultivate this gift? There are many things said in the scriptures; I think particularly of two verses in the fourth chapter of Mosiah wherein King Benjamin summarizes exactly what we must do if we want the gift of the Holy Ghost as part of our lives and as an integral part of our communication process:

> Believe in God; believe that he is, and that he created all things, both in heaven and in earth; believe that he has all wisdom, and all power, both in heaven and in earth; [and this next line is especially important] believe that man doth not comprehend all things which the Lord can comprehend (Mosiah 4:9).

In other words, we must have faith in God for that which we do not know or understand. He continues: "And again, believe that ye must repent of your sins and forsake them, and humble yourselves before God; and ask in sincerity of heart that he would forgive you; and now if you believe in all these things see that ye do them" (Mosiah 4:10).

I believe that the power of the gift of the Holy Ghost is withheld from some of us because we lack faith in it. The Lord has told us that we have not because we ask not. And I believe that sometimes this gift, which would strengthen us and help us and lead us to truth, is limited in our lives simply because we do not seek it, because we do not ask for it. I believe that when we do ask for it, influences are set in motion that will draw us toward light and truth, help us to know things as they are, and finally make the process of communication accurate and true.

Fortunately, the Lord has provided us with a pattern for asking for and receiving the gift of the Spirit.

James issues the familiar challenge, "If any of you lack wisdom, let him ask of God, that giveth to all men liberally, and upbraideth not; and it shall be given him" (James 1:5). For the person who finds it hard to take even the first step, we have the following from Alma:

> But behold, if ye will . . . arouse your faculties, even to an experiment upon my words, and exercise a particle of faith, yea, even if ye can no more than desire to believe, let this desire work in you, even until ye believe in a manner that ye can give place for a portion of my words.
>
> Now, we will compare the word unto a seed. Now, if ye give place, that a seed may be planted in your heart, behold, if it be a true seed, or a good seed, if ye do not cast it out by your unbelief, that ye will resist the Spirit of the Lord, behold, it will begin to swell within your breasts; and when you feel these swelling motions, ye will begin to say within yourselves—It must needs be that this is a good seed, or that the word is good, for it beginneth to enlarge my soul; yea, it beginneth to enlighten my understanding, yea, it beginneth to be delicious to me. . . .
>
> And now, behold, because ye have tried the experiment, and planted the seed, and it swelleth and sprouteth, and beginneth to grow, ye must needs know that the seed is good.
>
> And now, behold, is your knowledge perfect? Yea, your knowledge is perfect in that thing, and your faith is dormant; and this because you know, for ye know that the word hath swelled your souls, and ye also know that it hath sprouted up, that your understanding doth begin to be enlightened, and your mind doth begin to expand. (Alma 32:27–28, 33–34.)

Thus we see that the Lord has provided a way for anyone to experiment on his words.

The Lord also said: "Ye shall know them by their fruits. Do men gather grapes of thorns, or figs of thistles?" (Matthew 7:16.)

The fascinating thing about this is that we do not necessarily have to take someone else's word for it; we can find out for ourselves by experimenting on the words of the Lord. There are some, I am sure, who will say that this might be akin to talking oneself into something. I would say to them that if they feel this way, to keep the thought in mind, but nonetheless follow the pattern and experiment on the words and find out for themselves. No honest searcher for truth will reject the words without the experiment.

The question then arises, upon what shall we experiment? Let me mention a few specifics.

The Lord has instituted the law of tithing. Have we fully complied with this law in order to understand what the Lord has in store for those who obey it?

The same is true of the Word of Wisdom, keeping the Sabbath day holy, and all other principles and ordinances of the Church. They represent opportunities to find out what blessings are available to those who comply with the Lord's teachings. After sacrament meeting, for instance, is Sunday like any other day, or have we unlocked the true blessings of the Sabbath?

Finally, from the Doctrine and Covenants we read these words:

> And the Book of Mormon and the holy scriptures are given of me for your instruction; and the power of my Spirit quickeneth all things (D&C 33:16).
> And those who receive it in faith, and work righteousness, shall receive a crown of eternal life (D&C 20:14).

I bear witness that the Lord Jesus Christ, Savior of all the earth, means what He says: that those who receive this book in faith and work righteousness will gain eternal life; that the Lord loves and cares for each of His children and would have them all return to Him.

May we all accept His invitation and find out for ourselves. May we realize that the true academic approach, the search for pure truth, is in harmony with what the Lord would have us do. May the Lord help us in our search for truth. And may we seek the Holy Spirit so that we may know the truth, our understandings may be opened, and we may be increasingly enlightened.

A Second Witness for Christ

The Book of Mormon, that marvelous volume of scripture that makes us unique as a Church, serves as a bridge between a world that does not know man's eternal destiny and the revealed gospel of Jesus Christ. This bridge will bring us all closer to Deity by following its precepts. Those who seek to understand The Church of Jesus Christ of Latter-day Saints must start with a thoughtful reading of the Book of Mormon.

I would like to address my remarks to those who are not of this faith; and since we are all the children of God, I would like to refer to you as my brothers and sisters.

With the approach of the Easter season, the world takes note of the greatest event known to mankind. The literalness of the death, burial, and resurrection of Jesus Christ lifts him above the status of a great man or an inspired leader. To overcome death for all mankind, Jesus Christ had to be the Son of God and the Redeemer and Savior of the world.

To members of The Church of Jesus Christ of Latter-day Saints, this miraculous event has double meaning, for we have two sources to which we can look for an account of the resurrection. One, of course, is the Holy Bible. One cannot help but gain peace and reassurance from the words of John, which record, "Jesus said unto her, I am the resurrection, and the life: he that believeth in me, though he were dead, yet shall he live" (John 11:25); or the words of Mark which describe the experience of those going to the tomb after the death of the Savior:

Address given at general conference April 1973.

> And entering into the sepulchre, they saw a young man sitting on the right side, clothed in a long white garment; and they were affrighted.
>
> And he saith unto them, Be not affrighted: Ye seek Jesus of Nazareth, which was crucified: he is risen; he is not here: behold the place where they laid him. (Mark 16:5–6.)

After these experiences in the land of the Bible, another people in a far-off land, a remnant of the house of Israel who also had prophets and kept their own scriptural record, recorded the following concerning the resurrected Lord:

> And it came to pass, as they understood they cast their eyes up again toward heaven; and behold, they saw a Man descending out of heaven; and he was clothed in a white robe; and he came down and stood in the midst of them; and the eyes of the whole multitude were turned upon him, and they durst not open their mouths, even one to another, and wist not what it meant, for they thought it was an angel that had appeared unto them.
>
> And it came to pass that he stretched forth his hand and spake unto the people, saying:
>
> Behold, I am Jesus Christ, whom the prophets testified shall come into the world.
>
> And behold, I am the light and the life of the world; and I have drunk out of that bitter cup which the Father hath given me, and have glorified the Father in taking upon me the sins of the world, in the which I have suffered the will of the Father in all things from the beginning. (3 Nephi 11:8–11.)

A second evidence, then, is recorded to verify what was mentioned in the Holy Bible concerning the resurrection of the Savior. This second witness for Christ can be found in the volume of scripture known as the Book of Mormon. It is a compilation of the writings of the prophets of God who were part of the great civilization which lived anciently in the Americas. These prophets taught the gospel of Jesus Christ, as did their counterparts in the Holy Land, and they spoke of the birth and life of the Savior as well as His death and resurrection.

The highlight of this great record was the appearance of the resurrected Savior to these people and His teaching them the same gospel that He had presented to those who were His disciples in the Holy Land. It was only a matter of three generations from that time, however, that the people entirely rejected the teachings of Jesus Christ. They had become warlike and even rejected the prophets.

One of the last prophets to live among the Nephites was a man by the name of Mormon, who took all of the records and abridged them. For this reason the volume is known as the Book of Mormon. Mormon passed the sacred records to his son Moroni, who was one of the last followers of Christ in that generation, himself being a hunted man because of his beliefs. It was made known to Moroni and to other prophets that the Lord would bring this record forward in a later generation of time, to testify of the events that took place in Jerusalem and to convince mankind that Jesus Christ is the Son of God and that there is a plan whereby man can be saved and receive eternal life.

Being commanded of the Lord, the prophet Moroni buried the record in a hill, and there it remained until the year 1827, when a young man by the name of Joseph Smith was allowed by a divine messenger to take the record from where it was hidden and was given power to translate it so that the world might have a second evidence that the basic truths of the Bible are correct.

There were witnesses to the translation of these plates. In a joint statement Oliver Cowdery, David Whitmer, and Martin Harris gave the following testimony: "Be it known unto all nations, kindreds, tongues, and people, unto whom this work shall come: That we, through the grace of God the Father, and our Lord Jesus Christ, have seen the plates which contain this record. . . . And we also know that they have been translated by the gift and power of God, for his voice hath declared it unto us; wherefore we know of a surety that the work is true." (Book of Mormon: The Testimony of Three Witnesses.)

The reason for the Book of Mormon coming forth in this generation of time can be found on the title page of the book, which is part of the translated record and which says in part that the record was written "to the convincing of the Jew and Gentile that Jesus is the Christ, the Eternal God, manifesting himself unto all nations." The Book of Mormon, then, is a means whereby men can be convinced that God lives and that Jesus Christ is His son and the Savior of the world.

This book, then, bears record of the divine Sonship of Jesus

Christ and recognizes Him as Redeemer of the world. This passage from 3 Nephi in the Book of Mormon is a good example:

> Behold, I am Jesus Christ the Son of God. I created the heavens and the earth, and all things that in them are. . . .
>
> Behold, I have come unto the world to bring redemption unto the world, to save the world from sin.
>
> Therefore, whoso repenteth and cometh unto me as a little child, him will I receive, for of such is the kingdom of God. Behold, for such I have laid down my life, and have taken it up again; therefore repent, and come unto me ye ends of the earth, and be saved. (3 Nephi 9:15, 21–22.)

A second message of the Book of Mormon is to teach mankind the plan of salvation in its pure and basic form so that we might know what the Lord expects of us in order to be saved. Again, an example of this can be found from the words of the Savior in 3 Nephi:

> And this is my doctrine, and it is the doctrine which the Father hath given unto me; . . . and I bear record that the Father commandeth all men, everywhere, to repent and believe in me.
>
> And whoso believeth in me, and is baptized, the same shall be saved; and they are they who shall inherit the kingdom of God. (3 Nephi 11:32–33.)

At the same time the Savior spoke these words, He also commissioned certain disciples with specific authority to perform the baptism just spoken of. He also explained what He meant by repentance and what steps must be taken in order to gain this repentance.

And finally, if the Book of Mormon is true, then it must attest to the fact that Joseph Smith, the translator of this record, was a prophet of God and was divinely inspired to bring forth this work. In the revelation concerning the coming forth of the Book of Mormon the Lord referred to Joseph Smith in the following way: "He has translated the book, even that part which I have commanded him, and as your Lord and your God liveth it is true" (D&C 17:6).

Joseph Smith once made the statement that the Book of Mormon was the keystone of this religion, that a person could get closer to God by following its precepts than by any other book. Joseph Smith has long since passed away. But The Church of Jesus Christ of Latter-day Saints and the Book of Mormon live on as a sign and witness to all nations that Jesus Christ is the Son of God, that there is a way to return to the presence of God, and that the basic truths of the Holy Bible are correct.

Realizing that there would be those who might say, "Yes, but how can we know?" The last prophet to write in the book gave this promise:

> Behold, I would exhort you that when ye shall read these things, if it be wisdom in God that ye should read them, that ye would remember how merciful the Lord hath been unto the children of men, from the creation of Adam even down until the time that ye shall receive these things, and ponder it in your hearts.
>
> And when ye shall receive these things, I would exhort you that ye would ask God, the Eternal Father, in the name of Christ, if these things are not true; and if ye shall ask with a sincere heart, with real intent, having faith in Christ, he will manifest the truth of it unto you, by the power of the Holy Ghost.
>
> And by the power of the Holy Ghost ye may know the truth of all things. (Moroni 10:3–5.)

This promise is made, then, to all who want to know, that if they will read these things and ponder them in their hearts and do it prayerfully, the truth will be made known unto them.

Today, the Church is known as The Church of Jesus Christ of Latter-day Saints, to distinguish it from the Church of Jesus Christ that existed at the time of the New Testament and the Book of Mormon.

As in the ancient Church, it has Apostles and prophets at the head, and it teaches that all mankind can be saved through obedience to the principles and ordinances of the gospel of Jesus Christ.

We believe that the Savior literally leads His church through direct and continuous revelation to its leaders. We believe, too, that all mankind are the sons and daughters of God, and that if they will prayerfully and honestly seek Him, He will bless them with a realization of the truthfulness of these things. We believe that Jesus Christ will come again to the earth, and when He does, He will reign as King of kings, as the resurrected Lord, and as the Prince of Peace.

To this I bear my humble witness. I know that God lives and that Jesus Christ is His Son, and that this work is true, for the Lord God has revealed it to me. And since we are all the children of God, we all have a right to this knowledge.

Reason, the Spirit, and the Search

The true role of the leader or the teacher in this Church is to turn the hearts of the people to the Lord. When this happens, a way is opened to establish truth and dispel doubt. We are a "come and see" religion seeking to turn people to the Lord rather than trying to persuade them to believe through attractive and cleverly worded presentations.

A few years ago I corresponded with a Church member who was disturbed because Church leaders had made some strong statements about the particular field he had trained for and in which he was now teaching. In fact, I had made reference to some of these statements (from the leaders) in answering a question in a Church meeting that he had attended, which had distressed him considerably.

I soon regretted my decision to correspond with him as he gradually moved me into his area of expertise. I had some superficial knowledge of what he was speaking about, but I was no match against someone who had been well trained in the principles and theories of his field.

Realizing my predicament, I gradually turned the correspondence back to a gospel orientation by asking my friend some pointed questions that dealt with the Spirit's role in the decision-making process of a Latter-day Saint. He answered me with sincerity, using the words that a Latter-day Saint would be expected to use. But I also noticed that he tended to talk more about past prophets and their writings, avoiding what Church leaders were saying today. And always he wanted to get back to the theoretical issues surrounding his discipline.

I concluded from our correspondence, as I understood it, that there was something missing from his experience with the gospel. I gradually realized that, just as I had only a superficial knowledge of his field, so had he been superficial about the spiritual realm of his religion. He knew the words, but there was something missing. He knew the gospel, but he had not fully partaken of it. He had not been "born of the Spirit," as the scripture says.

Our correspondence suddenly halted. My friend was frustrated that I didn't know enough about his discipline, and I was anguished because I knew there were ways open to him to resolve his problems—ways that he did not entirely understand or was not willing to admit.

There is a way provided for all members of the Church to come to an understanding of doctrines, procedures, and the pronouncements of Church leaders. It has been integral to the Church since the very beginning and is referred to constantly by our leaders. Yet too many Church members neglect to use it. Some prefer instead to search out statements made by past leaders to support a position that may not be in harmony with what Church leaders are saying today. Some seek out statements that appear contradictory or confusing, and use this to justify their own contrary point of view. "If past leaders did not agree," they reason, "why should I be bound to agree with what is said today?" Still others seek to be commanded in all things. They seek for and sometimes demand a First Presidency statement before they can resolve a matter in their minds.

While these approaches may have some value, there is another way open to all within the kingdom. It is designed to get at truth, resolve differences, and confirm to each individual what the Lord wants him to do. It is a way that is often discussed, but not always used by Latter-day Saints.

It is personal revelation.

"The Holy Ghost is a revelator," said the Prophet Joseph Smith. "No man can receive the Holy Ghost without receiving revelation" (*History of the Church,* 6:58).

Far better than someone else telling us what is right or wrong—or telling us how to resolve an issue—is our right to go before the throne of truth and seek to resolve that which is not clear. We can use personal revelation to capture the spirit of what comes to us by those whom the Lord has called to give His church direction. While it is contrary to the order of heaven to receive revelation for one higher in authority in the Lord's kingdom (see D&C 28:2–8), nevertheless, a person can have confirmed by the Spirit that which has come to the leader.

If a person presents himself before the Lord in the right way and perseveres, there is absolutely no doubt that whatever he needs to understand he will understand, and what he needs to know he will eventually know, and peace will come to his heart.

Approaching the throne of grace and truth and redeeming love is all-important. A perfect guide is provided in the words of King Benjamin. In a last great address to his people before his death, this God-fearing king taught them again the gospel of Jesus Christ, including some important words on the Atonement. He concluded by discussing conditions of salvation and citing a great truth about our dependence on the Lord. I offer it here because it is the only way a person can develop enough faith and humility to receive an answer from the Lord: "Believe in God; believe that he is, and that he created all things, both in heaven and in earth; believe that he has all wisdom, and all power, both in heaven and in earth; believe that man doth not comprehend all the things which the Lord can comprehend" (Mosiah 4:9).

Thus our challenge is to go before the Lord and accept Him as He really is: the Creator and Possessor of all wisdom and all power, who comprehends things that man cannot comprehend.

For some this may be difficult. They may feel they can seek the Lord's direction in this or that matter pertaining to Church or family, but to address him as the Possessor of *all* wisdom and *all* power? They may indeed be challenged to offer sincerely a prayer such as this: "I come before thee, Lord, because thou art the sole person who knows everything there is to know about my field of endeavor, my discipline, and all else about which I might have a question. I know that thou knowest more than I and all the people in my field, and I have come before thee not to counsel thee or to make a case for what I understand the truth to be, but to seek light and understanding. Give me knowledge and understanding so that I can resolve this matter in my heart.''

A person who can truly accept God in this light will know the beginning of the faith and humility that will unlock personal revelation on any matter he cares to bring before the Lord with belief and perseverance (see Mormon 9:27).

No matter what our position is, it is important that we go before the Lord and have faith in Him as the possessor of the ultimate answer. We should not divide our knowledge and say, ''These are the things I pray about, and these others I will work out only by reason and by the knowledge available in my field.'' Our God is all-powerful and all-knowing, and, as Joseph Smith said, our understanding of these attributes is the foundation of faith.

In a revelation given through President John Taylor, the Lord instructed the priesthood of the Church to ''humble themselves before me, and seek not their own will but my will [sometimes hard when we are committed to a point of view]; for if my priesthood, whom I have chosen, and called, and endowed with the spirit and gifts of their several callings, and with the power thereof, do not acknowledge me I will not acknowledge them, saith the Lord.'' (B.H. Roberts, *Life of John Taylor* [Salt Lake City: Bookcraft, 1963], pp. 350–51.)

To be acknowledged by the Lord and to receive an answer to our prayers, we must first acknowledge and honor Him as the ultimate in wisdom and knowledge and glory. Does this not bring with it a feeling of greater humility and profound faith? Such an approach, if pursued, will without question resolve differences, generate knowledge, and bring feelings of peace and unity to one's heart.

These feelings of divine confirmation can also be sought for and received as a confirmation of those in leadership positions.

Sometimes you find yourself serving with those whom, for one reason or another, you may have differences with. These differences are usually centered on personality and differences of opinion, not on doctrine or proper Church procedure. Some years ago I remember serving under a bishop, a good man, whom I had a hard time following. But I knew the Lord had called him, and prayerful efforts to seek a confirmation of that calling changed my feelings and helped me develop a love and respect for him.

President Spencer W. Kimball had this to say about sustaining:

> A person who judges anyone else is just as likely to judge his Church leaders, often thereby bringing disharmony and contention to our wards and branches. But the spirit of forgiveness and not of judgment is what is required—forgiveness and understanding. If those who seem so disturbed about the actions of their leaders would only pray to the Lord with full purpose of heart, saying constantly, "Thy will be done" and "Father, lead me aright and I will accept," their attitude would change and they would return to happiness and peace. (*The Miracle of Forgiveness* [Salt Lake City: Bookcraft, 1969], p. 268.)

King Benjamin gave us the first guide: to accept God as He actually is, and to go before Him with the faith and humility necessary for approaching someone who has all wisdom and power. We approach Him not to counsel Him, but to state our circumstances and present the matter before His throne. We state to Him where our deliberations and reasonings have brought us, and what we need in order to proceed. We should not demand or condemn, but seek truth, guidance, and inspiration from the Lord.

King Benjamin mentions a second qualification for obtaining personal revelation: "And again, believe that ye must repent of your sins and forsake them, and humble yourselves before God; and ask in sincerity of heart that he would forgive you" (Mosiah 4:10).

A person who wants and needs an answer to his prayers must bring himself in harmony with the commandments. He must be committed to the principles that the Lord has given His people to live by. Tithing, the Word of Wisdom, virtue—all the commandments help us to draw near to the Lord so that He can draw near to us. Seeking forgiveness from Him for our sins is a constant recognition of His supreme role and it will gain us forgiveness if we are truly humble and penitent.

King Benjamin's final expression is a telling one: "And now, if you believe all these things see that ye do them" (Mosiah

4:10). This is not just an academic exercise. It is an outlined procedure for us to follow; it is something to *do*. The whole structure of the gospel is designed to encourage people to enter into and develop an understanding of the Lord, a spiritual maturity. This is acquired not through the experiences of others, but by firsthand experiences conveyed by the Spirit. For this reason the gift of the Holy Ghost is conferred so that eventually "every man might speak in the name of God the Lord" (D&C 1:20).

Just as Philip told a questioning Nathanael to "come and see" if Jesus of Nazareth was not He of whom Moses wrote in the law and the prophets (see John 1:45–46), so the purpose of the Lord's church is to bring people to a true and personal testimony of the Lord. If two missionaries, for instance, are especially gifted in teaching the gospel to nonmembers, the one who is most effective in helping his investigator to "come and see" will always have the greatest success. The missionary who will present the principles, testify, and then help the investigator to develop his own program of meaningful prayer and study will be more successful than the missionary who will try to bear the burden of proof himself. If he feels that he must prove everything rather than have the investigator bear the burden of proof, he will not progress very far.

So it is with the entire Church. The Lord invites us to "come and see" for ourselves; to partake of His Spirit; to receive personal confirmation of that which is taught; to be at peace with the Church and its direction; to receive personal answers to our prayers and thereby gain knowledge and understanding. For us to accomplish this, the Lord counsels, "Keep my commandments; hold your peace; appeal unto my Spirit" (D&C 11:18).

It is important to understand that when we try to receive knowledge and understanding from the Lord, it must be on the basis of spiritual confirmation and not solely on the basis of our knowledge or what conclusions our intellect can draw, as valuable as that might be.

Paul went to great lengths to point out the differences between man's knowledge, wisdom, and understanding and the spiritual basis upon which the Lord reveals truth. "My speech," he said, "and my preaching was not with enticing words of man's wisdom, but in demonstration of the Spirit and of power; That your faith should not stand in the wisdom of men [to receive your answers or confirm your point of view], but in the power of God." (1 Corinthians 2:4–5.)

Later, he made the distinction even more pronounced: "Now we have received, not the spirit of the world, but the spirit which is of God; that we might know the things that are freely given to us of God. Which things also we speak, not in the words which man's wisdom teacheth, but which the Holy Ghost teacheth; comparing spiritual things with spiritual." (1 Corinthians 2:12–13.)

As a leader in the Church acts in his calling, as he gives a talk or provides some direction, then it can be expected that the Spirit will confirm what he has said.

To understand fully what has been said in such instances, a person also needs to cultivate and listen by the same Spirit. To try to receive a worldly or intellectual understanding or confirmation of something that has been prompted by the Spirit is like trying to link worldly things with spiritual instead of, as Paul says, comparing spiritual things with spiritual. "But," he adds, "the natural man receiveth not the things of the Spirit of God: for they are foolishness unto him: neither can he know them, because they are spiritually discerned" (1 Corinthians 2:14).

When we prayerfully seek to understand that which has been written or spoken by those whom the Lord has called to lead His people, we will understand and begin to resolve differences by seeking the Spirit to help us understand and resolve what now becomes a spiritual matter.

In modern revelation the Lord says, "Therefore, why is it that ye cannot understand and know, that he that receiveth the word by the Spirit of truth receiveth it as it is preached by the Spirit of truth. Wherefore, he that preacheth and he that receiveth, understand one another, and both are edified and rejoice together." (D&C 50:21–22.) When this does not happen, it is too often because people either fail to seek the Spirit concerning the specific doctrine taught or the divine calling involved, or they try to put worldly and intellectual interpretations on spiritual matters, becoming frustrated and sometimes lost.

God is the supreme possessor of knowledge in all fields. He

has invited us to come to Him in all things. The Holy Spirit will bring knowledge and understanding. The speaker and hearer will be edified, and peace and understanding will prevail.

Why do some enter into challenges, debates, and needless confrontation? Too often it is merely the outward expression of a frustrated heart—a heart that has not experienced the peace that comes from the spirit of understanding. The need, then, is to turn inward first and compare spiritual things with spiritual while seeking divine guidance. Indeed, the divine path to all truth and knowledge is to seek the Lord, keeping in mind the prophet Alma's inspired counsel:

> And now I would that ye would be humble, and be submissive and gentle; easy to be entreated; full of patience and long-suffering; being temperate in all things; being diligent in keeping the commandments of God at all times; asking for whatsoever things ye stand in need, both spiritual and temporal; always returning thanks unto God for whatsoever things ye do receive (Alma 7:23).

Drink of the Pure Water

Just as food and drink nourish the body, so the gospel nourishes the souls of all who partake, both young and old. One of the great evidences of the truthfulness of this work is simply what happens to a person who decides to live its principles. There are many life-styles in the world, but there is only one path that offers a fulness of spiritual nourishment.

Consider these words of the Savior as he spoke to the woman of Samaria at Jacob's well: "Whosoever drinketh of this water shall thirst again: But whosoever drinketh of the water that I shall give him shall never thirst; but the water that I shall give him shall be in him a well of water springing up into everlasting life." (John 4:13–14.)

What greater way to demonstrate the saving, healing principles of the gospel of Jesus Christ than to relate them to life-sustaining water—water that is essential for every human being in order to live! If the woman drank from her own well she would thirst again, but if she drank from the Savior's well and partook of the principles that he taught, she would never thirst again—her soul would be nourished and she would have eternal life.

We live in a complex and challenging world. Young and old seem to be going to and fro and in their own way drinking from different wells, searching for that water which will begin to feed their souls, that will quench some inner thirst.

Address given at general conference April 1971.

The youth who associate themselves with various causes, some popular, many designed to accomplish much good, and a few militant; the adult who can find no satisfaction in his vocation and perhaps finds only frustration in his marriage and emptiness in his life; the militant who spends his life bitterly denouncing what he is against but is never quite certain what he is for; the person who turns to drugs, perhaps even attempting to equate it with a spiritual experience, and then realizes that for every high there is some kind of dismal low—perhaps these people and many others act more from an inner need to satisfy a yearning soul than from the face value of that in which they are involved, however worthy it may be.

Even in Russia, where its people have drunk at the well of socialist morality for fifty years, there is an indication of a desire for something more nourishing. After studying religion in Russia today, the journalist Paul Wohl stated that "socialist morality has been accepted as the official yardstick of good behavior, but whether Soviet man is more harmonious than his predecessor is a moot question. A scientific outlook is there, but so is religion. Its comeback is a phenomenon which the ideologists of communism cannot explain and about which they prefer to remain silent." He further noted that the move toward religion is primarily sparked by young people.

The writer told of a simple Russian woman who received the visit of her neighbor, a young engineer-physicist. "I know you are a believer," said the engineer. "Can you tell me about God? The philosophy of dialectical materialism does not satisfy me. I would like to know the viewpoint of believers."

It is most interesting to note that there is something fundamental and basic in the makeup of man that would sooner or later turn him to his creator, provided he does not completely strangle this inclination through evil works or chronic unbelief, and provided he doesn't condition himself to settle for less by insisting that what he doesn't know or hasn't experienced just isn't so. Speaking of the Savior, the prophet Alma said: "Behold, he sendeth an invitation unto all men, for the arms of mercy are extended towards them, and he saith: Repent, and I will receive you. Yea, he saith: Come unto me and ye shall partake of the fruit of the tree of life: yea, ye shall eat and drink of the bread and the waters of life freely; . . . Behold I say unto you that the good shepherd doth call you; yea, and in his own name he doth call you, which is the name of Christ.'' (Alma 5:33–34, 38.)

And after Alma taught the people those things relative to the gospel of Jesus Christ and what they can do in order to nourish their souls, find peace, and prepare for eternal life, he then said: ''And now I, Alma, do command you in the language of him who hath commanded me, that ye observe to do the words which I have spoken unto you. I speak by way of command unto you that belong to the church; and unto those who do not belong to the church I speak by way of invitation, saying: Come and be baptized unto repentance, that ye also may be partakers of the fruit of the tree of life.'' (Alma 5:61–62.)

Thus, it is possible for a person to have the fruit of the tree of salvation readily available to him, but to no avail if he does not partake!

I am reminded of two young men who came in to see me some months ago. They had been recommended by their priesthood leaders. From the moment they stepped into the office, they began in a very sincere way questioning certain doctrines and teachings and procedures of the Church. Their attitude, however, was not antagonistic—they were sincerely looking for answers.

I asked them finally if their questions perhaps represented the symptoms of their problem and not the cause. Wasn't their real question whether this church is true? whether it is actually the Church of Jesus Christ? and whether it is led by divine revelation? The young men agreed that perhaps if they were sure of the answers to these questions, they could take care of the other questions that seemed to arise in their hearts.

I asked them if they were willing to participate in an experiment to determine in their own minds if the Church is true. They agreed to such an experiment. One of them appeared to be athletically inclined, and so I turned to him and asked, ''If you wanted to learn about the chemical properties of water, would you go to the local sports stadium and run four laps around the track?''

He said, ''Of course not.''

I asked, "Why not?"

He said, "The two are not related."

We then turned to Luke, chapter 6, verse 44, and read: "For every tree is known by his own fruit. For of thorns men do not gather figs, nor of a bramble bush gather they grapes."

I explained that if we are going to experiment with the things of Christ, then we are going to have to put these things to a spiritual test—a test that the Savior himself has outlined for all those who wish to know, a test of action.

I then asked them if they read the scriptures.

They said, "No."

I asked them if they prayed.

They said, "Not often."

I asked them if they kept the Word of Wisdom.

They said, "Occasionally."

I asked them if they went to church.

They said they'd stopped.

I asked them if they would be interested in a three-month experiment. They said they would try but were not anxious to commit themselves until they found out what I had in mind.

"During the next three months will you attend all your Church meetings and listen carefully to what is being said, even taking notes of the principal points being made by the teachers and how these points might apply to your lives?"

They thought for a moment and said they would.

"During the next three months will you reinstitute in your personal life prayer, night and morning, thanking God for the blessings you enjoy and asking Him to help you know if the Church is true and if the things you are doing are meaningful to your lives?"

One of these young men, who considered himself an agnostic, balked at this, but then he finally agreed to do it on the basis that for the sake of the experiment he would accept the premise that there is a God and would appeal to this God for the light and knowledge which he was seeking.

I asked them if for the next three months they would refrain from drinking, smoking, and drugs. Although this created some anxiety, they resolved to do it.

I asked them if for the next three months they would resolve to keep themselves morally clean and in harmony with the principles of virtue which the Savior taught. They said they would. And then I suggested they establish a schedule, on their own, to read the Book of Mormon from cover to cover during the next three months—a few pages each day, with a prayer at each reading that the Lord would bless them to know if the book is true and actually from Him. They agreed.

Anticipating what might happen, I said, "Now, if you feel disposed to tell your friends about this, probably their first comment will be 'Boy, has Brother Dunn snowed you.' You may even feel that way a time or two during this experiment, but don't let it keep you from doing what you have agreed to do. If you think that might be a problem, then keep it in the back of your mind, and go ahead and honestly experiment, and let this three-month experience speak for itself." I added, "If things go properly, you'll notice some by-products, such as a growing awareness and concern for your fellowman and greater appreciation and consideration for other people." They accepted the challenge and left.

Of course, what I really hoped for was the experience that every member has a right to enjoy and everyone else has the right to receive, and that is the knowledge of a personal testimony. I think Brigham Young described it best when he said:

> There is no other experience known to mortal man that can be compared with the testimony or witness of the Holy Ghost. It is as powerful as a two-edged sword and burns in the breast of man like a consuming fire. It destroys fear and doubt, leaving in their stead absolute, unqualified, and incontrovertible knowledge that a principle or thing is true. . . .
>
> This same testimony has sustained faithful saints to the present day and will be a lamp to their path forever. The effect of this testimony reaches above and beyond all physical or earthly things and makes relationship with God the Father a literal, pulsing fact. Every fiber of both body and spirit responds to the witness of that testimony and the soul knows and lives the truth.

And so to those who have tasted the water at many wells only to find that the unquenching thirst of the soul drives them on in search of that which will bring peace and nourishment to the heart—to you, whoever you are, member or nonmember—will you not come and drink from this well, and taste and experiment and see if you have not found the waters of life where you can drink and thirst no more but be full with the joy of the true knowledge of Jesus Christ and His teachings and the purpose of your own life?

I bear you my witness that I know God lives. I know He lives and that Jesus Christ is our Redeemer and His Son. Joseph Smith saw what he said he saw, and we have a prophet of God with us today. Come, drink with me the pure water of that witness.

How to Gain a Testimony

This church continues to grow because it is true and its teachings meet the inner needs of the people of this world. The gospel carries with it a spirit that comes from heaven and testifies to all of its truthfulness. All who wish to know can know.

In an area conference held in Mexico, President Harold B. Lee made this statement:

> The strength of the Church is not to be measured by the amount of money paid as tithing by faithful members, or by the number of the total membership of the Church, or the number of Church chapels and temple buildings.
>
> The real strength of the Church is to be measured by the individual testimonies to be found in the total membership of The Church of Jesus Christ of Latter-day Saints. (Mexico City Area Conference 1972.)

No matter what position a person holds in this church, there is one thing to which he is entitled, and that is a testimony of its truthfulness. Not only is it the right of every member to know for himself, but every soul on this earth can, if he desires, receive a spiritual witness that God the Father actually lives.

He can know that Jesus Christ is the Son of God the Father and gave up His life on the cross that we might live, and that He was resurrected to ascend on high to take His place on the right hand of God.

He can know that Joseph Smith was a true prophet, and that in reality he saw God the Father and His Son Jesus Christ, and

Address given at general conference October 1972.

that he became the legal administrator to restore the kingdom of God to the earth.

He can know that The Church of Jesus Christ of Latter-day Saints is the kingdom of God on earth, and that anyone who makes himself worthy for baptism, by faith in the Lord Jesus Christ and repentance, can gain entrance to that kingdom.

He can know that the Book of Mormon is true, and that a person can get closer to God by abiding by its precepts than by any other book (see *History of the Church,* 4:461).

And he can know that we have today a living oracle, a prophet of God who stands at the head of the Lord's church on the earth.

It is not enough to enter into a scholarly discourse on the merits of this declaration, or to accept or reject these claims with a wave of the hand. True strength, true peace of mind, true purpose in life comes when an individual, regardless of what others may think, puts himself in a position so that the Lord can reveal to him the absolute truth of these things.

It is an experience that defies description, at least to one who has not yet paid the price to receive it. It is the awakening of the mind and spirit to absolute truth. It is a revelation from God. It goes beyond what we can know and understand with our mortal senses. It is a testimony of the truthfulness of the gospel of Jesus Christ.

Around the world, literally hundreds of people are gaining this testimony each day. I heard one person speak just a few days ago. He was a new convert to the Church. He was a young man and he had a young family. He told how his life had changed—how the life of his whole family had changed. For the first time he knew what his relationship to God was and what the Lord expected of him. Because of this, he said that he was a better husband and father. He knew where he was going and could lead his family in a better way. But most of all he was just happy—happy with the quiet joy that fills the life of every truly converted person.

People who look at us from the outside can't understand what makes this church so alive and its people so faithful and devoted. President Lee provided an explanation in the statement I quoted earlier: "The real strength of the Church is to be measured by the individual testimonies to be found in the total membership of The Church of Jesus Christ of Latter-day Saints.''

The way in which a person can gain a testimony is clearly defined by the Lord.

First let me read from the title page of the Book of Mormon, where the Lord gives the reasons for bringing forth this book to the world. In the second paragraph we read that the book is brought forth ''also to the convincing of the Jew and Gentile that Jesus is the Christ, the Eternal God, manifesting himself unto all nations.''

So the purpose of the book is to convince the world, both Jew and Gentile, that ''Jesus is the Christ, the Eternal God, manifesting himself to all nations.''

Next we read in section 20 of the Doctrine and Covenants, wherein the Lord speaks of Joseph Smith and the Book of Mormon:

> God ministered unto him by an holy angel, . . .
> And gave unto him commandments which inspired him;
> And gave him power from on high, by the means which were before prepared, to translate the Book of Mormon;
> Which contains a record of a fallen people, and the fulness of the gospel of Jesus Christ to the Gentiles and to the Jews also; . . .
> Proving to the world that the holy scriptures are true, and that God does inspire men and call them to his holy work in this age and generation, as well as in generations of old. (D&C 20:6–9, 11.)

The Book of Mormon, then, has been brought forth to convince mankind that Jesus is the Christ, that the holy scriptures are true, and that God is again speaking through prophets as He did in ancient times.

The contents of the Book of Mormon, then, become the means whereby a person can put himself in harmony with the Spirit of the Lord so he can prove to himself and be convinced that these things are true.

How this should be accomplished is outlined by one of the last prophets to write in this ancient book of scripture. Some 421 years after the birth of Christ, the prophet Moroni, writing to the people of this generation, gave the following guidelines:

Behold, I would exhort you that when ye shall read these things, if it be wisdom in God that ye should read them, that ye would remember how merciful the Lord hath been unto the children of men, from the creation of Adam even down until the time that ye shall receive these things, and ponder it in your hearts.

And when ye shall receive these things, I would exhort you that ye would ask God, the Eternal Father, in the name of Christ, if these things are not true; and if ye shall ask with a sincere heart, with real intent, having faith in Christ, he will manifest the truth of it unto you, by the power of the Holy Ghost.

And by the power of the Holy Ghost ye may know the truth of all things. (Moroni 10:3–5.)

The three steps, then, in seeking a testimony of the truthfulness of the gospel from the Lord Himself, are to read, ponder, and pray with real intent and sincerity of heart.

If a person will prayerfully read the pages of this inspired book, carefully turn over in his mind what he has read, and constantly ask the question, "Could any man have written this book?", the promise of the Lord is that He "will manifest the truth of it unto you, by the power of the Holy Ghost."

If the world would accept this invitation, they would know for themselves the source of strength of The Church of Jesus Christ of Latter-day Saints, for, like all of us, they would have gone to the source and received their own testimony.

To those who by heritage find themselves members of the Church but perhaps are not sure of their own testimonies, I would suggest that it is no sin to admit to yourself that you do not know—if, in fact, you don't know. You will err, however, if you come to the realization that you don't know and then do nothing about it. Member or nonmember alike, any person who wants to know *can* know.

If at present you live by the faith and testimony of your parents and those around you, that is certainly all right. But seek to reach out and gain your own testimony so that you can stand on the strength of your own faith in the Lord. It will help you solve many of your problems, and it will bring peace to your heart.

I would hope that as Latter-day Saints we can strengthen each other in the way which the Lord provided, by bearing our testimonies often—at Church meetings, in gospel classes, even at fast and testimony meetings.

We should renew our efforts to express our testimonies and give something more than a passing reference to the truthfulness of the gospel. With the bearing of testimony comes the spirit of testimony, and all are edified.

Finally, may we as Latter-day Saint parents bear our testimonies to our children in the home—actually express to our children exactly what it is about the Church that we know to be true. If we think our children know of our testimonies just because they live in the same house with us, we are mistaken. We need to say the words so our families can feel the same spirit of testimony that we have felt. Family home evening is an ideal time for us to share our feelings.

And may I add that the family setting is also an ideal place to read the Book of Mormon. As a family, we recently finished reading the Book of Mormon. Although two of our children are not old enough to read yet, we find that they understand more than we thought they would; for the spirit and truth of this great book enlighten people of all ages.

What greater inheritance can parents give their children than the spiritual heritage which the children have a right to receive?

To all people, both member and nonmember, comes an invitation from the God of this earth to learn for themselves the truth. May all who have not received that knowledge accept this invitation from the Savior of us all.

V.
To All
Nations

Is it not time that we listen to a prophet's voice? Is it not time that we lengthen our stride? Is it not time to teach the gospel of the kingdom to the world, and to our neighbor? I bear witness to you that the time has indeed come for us to be numbered among the faithful laborers in God's kingdom.

A Living Prophet

The advantage of having a living prophet is that we might know the Lord's mind and will concerning us, as a people, today. The holy scriptures are filled with the teachings, admonitions, and commandments of God, and we are most blessed to have such guidance. But the greatest gift of all is to have in our midst a living prophet. Each of us has the opportunity to know what the Lord expects of us today as we defer to the counsel of the living prophet.

Out of curiosity, I went back in the records of the Church to see what kind of attention the centennial of the nation received at the April general conference of 1876. Not much was said, but I did come across what would have to be considered the most spectacular unscheduled centennial event of that year.

It seems that on April 5, 1876, just one day before general conference started, four powder magazines located on Arsenal Hill exploded. The hill was located one mile north and east of the temple block, and the explosion of an estimated forty tons of powder scattered bits of stone and concrete all over the city and could be heard for miles around. It was reported that some thought the "day of judgment" had come—and I suspect this event had some impact on the number of people who attended the opening session of general conference the following day.

Among the teachings that caught my eye at that April 1876 conference were these words from Elder Wilford Woodruff:

Address given in general conference April 1976.

It may be asked—What are the commandments of the Lord? Many of them are contained in these records, the Bible, Book of Mormon, and Book of Doctrine and Covenants; and we have the living oracles with us, and have had from the commencement. The Lord will never leave his kingdom without a lawgiver, leader, president, . . . to direct the affairs of his Church on the earth, for the reason that it is the dispensation of the fulness of times, in which God has set up a kingdom which is to be an everlasting kingdom, and to whose dominion there will be no end. (*Journal of Discourses,* 18:189.)

That statement caused me to reflect on the absolute importance of a living oracle, and also on the words of Elder Orson F. Whitney of the Council of the Twelve, who said:

The Latter-day Saints do not do things because they happen to be printed in a book. They do not do things because God told the Jews to do them; nor do they do or leave undone anything because of instructions that Christ gave to the Nephites. Whatever is done by this church is because God, speaking from heaven in our day, has commanded this church to do it. No book presides over this church and no books lie at its foundation. You cannot pile up books enough to take the place of God's priesthood, inspired by the power of the Holy Ghost. (Conference Report, October 1916.)

Elder Whitney was not taking away from the power and majesty of the scriptures. He was just putting things into perspective. He also said:

No men ought to contend for what is in the books, in the face of God's mouthpiece, who speaks for him, and interprets His word. To contend is to defer to the dead letter in preference to the living oracles, which is always a false position. (Conference Report, October 1916.)

What is the Lord's oracle saying to us today? The general theme is to lengthen our stride in a variety of areas. I had the opportunity of accompanying President Spencer W. Kimball and other Brethren of the Church to the area general conference in the South Pacific. May I share with you some of what President Kimball said at those gatherings regarding missionary work.

In Apia, Samoa, he promised the Saints that if they would hold family home evening and see that baptisms, ordinations to the priesthood, missions, and temple marriages were carried out, the Lord would truly bless the people and very few would be lost.

In Hamilton, New Zealand, he called on the Saints to start a new effort to reach nonmembers all over the world. We are all called to warn our neighbors, he said, and we should not go back to our Maker without having properly done so.

In Tonga, President Kimball asked that we pray to the Lord to open up the nations of the world so that we can teach the gospel everywhere. He said he believed that if we as a Church petitioned the Lord night and morning to change the hearts of men and open the nations of the world, the Lord would intervene and open the way whereby we can teach the gospel to all nations.

In Sydney, Australia, he told of his throat operation and explained that the surgeons left a portion of the vocal cords, which allowed him to preach the gospel throughout the world. He said he wanted to continue to work very hard at doing this, but he doesn't want to do it alone. He then invited the members of the Church to stand with him and preach the gospel just as the Lord has commanded us to do. Concerning missionary work, he said that many young men who thought they didn't have to go or couldn't go are now finding that if they plan and prepare, they can indeed go. And then he said that they certainly should go.

In Brisbane, Australia, President Kimball said that as a church we must go forward, month in and month out, until we have brought the gospel to everyone.

In Tahiti he urged us to do missionary work and to send our boys on missions. He said that we must be serious about the missionary effort.

I think we all recognize these missionary messages, for he has repeated them many times. The only thing left to be done is to follow the prophet.

President Kimball's visit to Australia was the second official visit of a President of the Church to that country. The first was by President David O. McKay in 1955. When President McKay was in Brisbane, the mission president took him out one day to see the city. During the course of the day they were looking across the Brisbane River into a new subdivision which was known as Chermside. President McKay asked the mission president, "Do we have any missionaries in that area?" The mission president said no. President McKay then said, "Send the missionaries in, for the people are ready." Missionaries were sent into the area and they enjoyed tremendous success. Today, Chermside is part of the Brisbane Fourth Ward of the Brisbane Stake. These are the kinds of blessings that come when people not only listen to the living oracle but do what he says. The blessings are found in doing the word, not just in hearing the word.

The Church today is responding to a prophet. President Kimball has asked every worthy and able young man to go into the mission field, and because of this we now have great numbers of missionaries in the field. And the need is still great. Because he has asked every family in the Church prayerfully to friendship a nonmember family and otherwise to help the missionary effort, there are great numbers of converts coming into the Church. But still the prophet asks that more be done.

Thank God for the scriptures, which help us to grow in the gospel of Jesus Christ and to understand the nature and will of the Lord. But most of all, thank God for a living oracle, a legal administrator, so that we can know what the Lord wants us to do today. Under his direction we can have the legal right to act in the name of God so the gospel of Jesus Christ can be a living, viable influence built on current revelation.

Truly, "We thank Thee, O God, for a prophet, to guide us in these latter days."

Faithful Laborers

Each generation gives birth to unsung heroes who answer a call from the Lord and pay whatever price is required to help establish the gospel of Jesus Christ in the world. Most of those sacrifices are made by ordinary people as they go about their callings in the far-flung countries of the world.

We have been asked by a prophet to lengthen our stride in two general areas. First, every member of the Church needs to let his light so shine that others will see the gospel of Jesus Christ by example.

> And again, I say unto you, I give unto you a commandment, that every man, both elder, priest, teacher, and also member, go to with his might, with the labor of his hands, to prepare and accomplish the things which I have commanded.
>
> And let your preachings be the warning voice, every man to his neighbor, in mildness and in meekness. (D&C 38:40–41.)

To meet this need, every family in the Church is asked to friendship a nonmember family on a family-to-family basis.

Second, every able young man has been asked to prepare himself to serve a full-time mission.

> Wherefore lay to with your might and call *faithful* laborers into my vineyard, that it may be pruned for the last time.
>
> And inasmuch as they do repent and receive the fulness of my gospel, and become sanctified, I will stay my hand in judgment.
>
> Wherefore, go forth, crying with a loud voice, saying: The kingdom of heaven is at hand; crying: Hosanna! blessed be the name of the Most High God.

Address given at general conference April 1975.

Go forth baptizing with water, preparing the way before my
face for the time of my coming;

For the time is at hand; the day or the hour no man knoweth;
but it surely shall come. (D&C 39:17–21; emphasis added.)

I would like to enlarge on the second of these general areas. I
had the honor several years ago of being assigned to visit the
Samoa Apia Mission and attend some stake conferences in that
country. I found the missionaries all well and the work
progressing. One afternoon following our meeting, the mission
president, Patrick Peters, a native Samoan, said, "Elder Dunn,
there is something I'd like to show you." We drove a few miles
from the mission home, and climbed a small hill to a place that
was isolated by palm trees and other tropical vegetation. I suddenly realized that we were in a very old graveyard. At the
center of this graveyard was a plot surrounded by a cement wall
low enough to step over. President Peters told me this was
where some of the first missionaries in Samoa were buried.
There were eight graves.

The thing that struck my interest most was that out of eight
graves, four were for children under the age of two, and one was
for a twenty-one-year-old wife and mother. What role could
these have possibly played in missionary work in Samoa?

During the next two days, when time would permit, I
searched the mission's history for an answer. While I was
unable to gather information on all of the eight, I did discover
the following.

In the early days of the Church it was common for young
married couples to be called on missions, and some of these
young couples were called to Samoa. The first person to be
buried in that plot was Sister Katie Eliza Hale Merrill. She and
her husband had been in the mission for only three months
when she took sick and gave birth to a premature child. The
child died the next day. The history records: "An hour after the
death of the child, the mother called Sister Lee [wife of the
mission president] to her bedside and after thanking her for
waiting on her during the sickness, said that she was 'going to
die' and that she 'could not stay because they had come for her.'
She then talked with her husband, kissed him goodbye, and all
was over. The mother and baby boy were buried in one coffin."

After his mission, Brother Merrill took the remains of his wife and infant son back to Utah for burial.

Elder Thomas H. Hilton and Sister Sarah M. Hilton were serving a mission in Samoa, where they lost three of their children between 1891 and 1894. Little Jeanette lived less than a year, George Emmett for only seven days, and Thomas Harold for a year and a half. Of the death of Thomas Harold the record says:

> On Sunday the 11th, he was not feeling very well. . . . For two days following he appeared to be improving, but on the morning of the 14th, his mother again became concerned about his welfare. From then until his death, on March 17, 1894, everything that loving hands could do was done for his recovery, but he grew rapidly worse. . . .
>
> On how loth we all were to believe that it was so! How sad to see our dear sister *again* bereft, and her so far from dear parents and friends who she has left for the gospel's sake.
>
> Thomas Harold Hilton was about one and a half years old, a beautiful little boy and very dearly beloved by all the missionaries, as well as the natives who knew him. Much sympathy is felt for the bereaved parents and the blessings of the Lord are invoked upon them.

At twenty-nine, Ransom Stevens was president of the Samoa Mission when he was stricken with typhoid fever complicated by a heart problem. He died April 23, 1894. His widow, Sister Annie D. Stevens, started for home by steamer on May 23. She reached Ogden on Sunday, June 10, where she was met by President Joseph F. Smith and Elder Franklin D. Richards. On June 11 she had an interview with the First Presidency in Salt Lake City, and then went on to her home in Fairview, Sanpete County, arriving at 6:00 P.M.

The history states that "greetings by her friends were necessarily brief, for Sister Stevens was ill and had to retire to bed early, and at 11 P.M., five hours after her arrival home, she gave birth to a nice boy." She had gone through the whole ordeal in the advanced stages of pregnancy.

Friday, March 2, 1900: "Little Loi Roberts was given up to die by Dr. Stuttaford at the sanatorium [in Apia]. The patient little sufferer was adminstered to daily and each time he would get relief. . . . His parents [Elder and Sister E. T. Roberts] were untiring in their efforts to allay pain and sufferings.''

Saturday, March 3: "Little Loi died at the sanatorium in Apia in the morning, making another sad day in the history of the mission.'' Small wonder that the tombstone contained the words, "Rest, sweet Loi, rest.'' He was one-and-a-half years old.

And that brings us to Elder William A. Moody and his bride, Sister Adelia Moody. They were called on a mission from Thatcher, Graham County, Arizona, arriving in Samoa in November 1894. They must have had the same hopes and aspirations of any young couple just starting out. She gave birth to an eight-pound daughter on May 3, 1895. Three weeks later Adelia passed away. The daughter, little Hazel Moody, was cared for by local Saints while her father continued his mission. Finally, one year later a steamer left for the United States; the passengers included four returning elders and "also Elder Moody's daughter, Hazel, one year old, who will be delivered to loving relatives in Zion.''

A price has been paid for the establishment of the gospel of Jesus Christ in the land of Samoa. It is interesting to note that much of that price was paid by little children. I suspect that there are many obscure cemeteries in many nations of the world similar to that little plot in Samoa. They are a mute witness of the trials and suffering that went into the beginnings of missionary work in this dispensation.

Because of advancements in the standard of living and medical technology, these kinds of trials are almost a thing of the past. In Samoa, for instance, I found the missionaries well. There are even health missionaries, including a young couple and their two children who are helping to improve the health standards of the members and looking after the health of the missionaries where needed.

The sacrifice today is mostly one of time and money—sacrifice of twenty-four months for a worthy young man to help move the Lord's cause forward. Others gave their lives to get the work started, but today the Lord requires only that we sacrifice some time and our means to keep His work moving throughout the world.

The story is told that toward the end of World War II an allied general came to the front lines one night to inspect his troops. As he walked along he would point out into no-man's land and say, "Can you see them? Can you see them?"

Finally someone said, "General, we can see nothing. What do you mean?" He said, "Can't you see them? They're your buddies; they are the ones who gave their lives today, yesterday, and the day before. They're out there all right, watching you, wondering what you are going to do—wondering if they died in vain."

As members of this Church, we can ask ourselves the same question: "Can you see them?" They are the ones who paid so dearly, some with their lives, so that the gospel of the kingdom might be established in these, the last days. They are the Hiltons, and the Robertses, and the Stevenses, and the Moodys, and many others. They are people like you and me who answered a call from God. I am sure they are allowed to look in on us from time to time to see how this work is going, to see what we are doing with their spiritual heritage, to see if they died in vain.

I wonder, young men, how successful you would be in convincing a young father who, because of the gospel of Jesus Christ, has buried three of his babies in an obscure graveyard halfway around the world, that a mission is too much of a sacrifice because you want to buy a car or a stereo, or because you don't want to interrupt your schooling, or for some other reason.

As members of the Church, I wonder how convincing we would be in telling someone that we are just too busy, and maybe just a little embarrassed, to share the gospel with our neighbor—especially if that someone were a young father who had buried his bride while on his mission and sent his little girl home to be taken care of by relatives while he finished his service to the Lord.

Is it not time that we listen to a prophet's voice? Is it not time that we lengthen our stride? Is it not time to teach the gospel of the kingdom to the world, and to our neighbor? I bear witness to you that the time has indeed come for us to be numbered among the faithful laborers in God's kingdom.

Sharing the Gospel

We frequently look to the headquarters of the Church for strength and guidance, but as the Church expands throughout the nations of the earth, some of the greatest examples of faith and most promising opportunities for service can often be found away from the center of the Church.

I cannot think of New Zealand and its Saints without thinking of great faith. I recall when I was assigned to some stake conferences in New Zealand some time ago. We had just finished a meeting in which the subject was the payment of tithes and the Lord's blessings for those who are tithe payers. Following the meeting one of the priesthood leaders came up and related to me how the Lord had blessed him because he had paid his tithes. He explained how his small construction business had failed and had left him deeply in debt. His bookkeeper had told him that he must stop making the monthly contribution to his church, which, of course, was tithing. This faithful member then told the bookkeeper that if he was ever to get out of his financial problems he would need the help of the Lord, and that a full and honest tithe was the way for that help to come.

He then told me how, step by step, the Lord began to bless him by opening up opportunities that allowed him to get out of his financial difficulties. In the beginning he had even lost his house, but he was able to do a job for someone who could not pay him. The man, however, did have a vacant house, and so

Address given at Hamilton, New Zealand Area Conference February 1976.

this member and his family were allowed to stay there free of rent for a number of months.

Later, he was able to buy a tractor for a very good price because it had become bogged down in mud, but he would have to get it out of the mud himself. Somehow he was able to do this, and he was back in business.

He told of cutting down a large tree one day in the course of his work, and how, after the tree was cut, it did not fall. He stood by the tree, looking at it and saying to himself, "Why don't you fall?" A voice came into his mind which said, "Because you are standing in the way." He moved a few feet and the tree came crashing down right where he had stood, destroying the hand tools that were by his side. This brother bore fervent testimony that the Lord sometimes blesses the honest tithe payer in unexpected ways.

There is another area of Church activity that we would ask all to support with their faith, prayers, and actions.

Let us first turn to the Doctrine and Covenants to find out what this important opportunity is. The Lord tells us:

> And again, I say unto you, I give unto you a commandment, that every man, both elder, priest, teacher, and also member, go to with his might, with the labor of his hands, to prepare and accomplish the things which I have commanded.
>
> And let your preaching be the warning voice, every man to his neighbor, in mildness and in meekness. (D&C 38:40–41.)

First, the Lord tells us that what He is about to give us is a commandment—not a suggestion or an idea, but a divine commandment.

Second, He tells us that this commandment includes every member: "every man, both elder, priest, teacher, and also member." Think of it—the Lord is asking all of us to unite to accomplish His work.

Third, He says that we must "go to with [our] might" and "with the labor of [our] hands." In other words, it is something that we should not just talk about, but something that He actually wants us to do with our own efforts and determination.

And fourth, He tells us what He wants us to do: "Let your preaching be the warning voice, every man to his neighbor, in mildness and in meekness."

What a marvelous opportunity we have to share the gospel of Jesus Christ, to share the things that have brought us all so much happiness and peace of mind, to share the blessings of eternal family unity! All people are children of our loving Heavenly Father, and He has asked each of us to go to our neighbor in mildness and meekness—not arguing, but in peace and love and friendship—to let our neighbors see by our lives, by what we say and do, that this is truly the gospel of Jesus Christ.

This means, then, that we as members often have more influence as far as missionary work is concerned than full-time missionaries do. The Lord extends a marvelous opportunity to accept His commandment and begin to prepare the lives of our friends and associates for the beauties of this wonderful gospel of Jesus Christ. So let's do it in cooperation with the missionaries.

One member accepted this responsibility and went about fulfilling it in this way. First, he gathered his family together in a family home evening and explained to them what the Lord had asked each member of the Church to do. The family then prayerfully chose a nonmember family with whom they were acquainted and whose friendship they enjoyed.

This man then went to see the head of that family and invited the whole family over to a family party. When the family came over and they began to talk, the member father became quite bold and made this statement: "I'm so pleased with what my church does to help each member of my family to grow and develop that if you would like to ask any question about this church, I will have my eleven-year-old boy answer it for you." He said he knew he had gone too far when his son mumbled something like, "Thanks a lot, Dad." However, the boy did answer the question, and the relationship between the two families progressed from that time forward.

On one occasion the nonmember father said, "Why do we always talk about your church and never talk about my church?" The member said, "That's a good point. For every five minutes we talk about my church, we'll talk ten minutes about yours." The man then began to talk about his church, and the member father listened attentively. However, after six or seven minutes the man looked at the member and said, "You know, I can't think of anything more to say."

As a result of this family-to-family friendshipping the entire family was baptized, and there was no one filled with greater joy than this member and his family. Here now were two families in the gospel of Jesus Christ.

This type of activity is going on all over the world because a living prophet has reemphasized the Lord's commandment to preach the gospel. He has asked every family in the Church to (1) prayerfully choose one or more nonmembers; (2) have regular and appropriate friendshipping experiences with them; and (3) report their progress to their ward or branch mission leaders.

What joy comes to the heart of the person who is able to bring to his fellowmen one of the greatest gifts of all, even a knowledge of the truthfulness of the gospel of Jesus Christ! If every family in this congregation today were to share the gospel in this manner, according to the commandment of the Lord in the Doctrine and Covenants, what a blessing it would be. Think of how many more good strong families there would be to help build the kingdom of God.

Let me quote from a talk given by Elder Matthew Cowley:

> There is no greater joy than taking this gospel to your neighbor. People want to hear about religion today. They are in trouble. They don't know what is going to happen next. The world is full of confusion. . . . If you want to have something come into your lives that will fill you with faith through all eternity, get into this missionary work and get the spirit of it, and joy will come into your heart, and people will hold your names in remembrance to the end of time." (*Matthew Cowley Speaks* [Deseret Book, 1954], p. 409.)

Let me turn now to another phase of missionary work. Every young man of suitable age who has come into the kingdom through the waters of baptism, and who has had the priesthood bestowed upon him, and who is worthy and able, has been asked by the Church to prepare for missionary service. To all who fall within these guidelines, the prophet has extended the invitation to prepare to serve the Lord in this capacity. What a marvelous opportunity it offers us to follow the prophet!

Finances will have to be arranged for, but this will be possible if the young man and his family and the local quorum begin to plan early for the mission experience. Let me share with you the experience of one father to demonstrate what faith and determination can do. His missionary son writes:

> My sister recently went on a mission to one of the missions in the States and my father knew he would have trouble keeping both of us out so he went to the bishop and asked for a blessing so he would be able to do so. The bishop said, "That won't be necessary, we can just get the elders quorum to keep one of them out till the other comes home and then you can take care of it." My father said, "That isn't what I want. I want to keep them out. You just give me a blessing so I can." The bishop sat him down and gave him a blessing. The next Monday when he went to work there was a check on his desk for $1,000 with a note from his employer saying, "We appreciate your services and dedication. Please accept this token of our appreciation."

The Lord will not bless everyone in just this way, but He will help those who plan and sacrifice and have determination to find ways and means for missionary service.

Our challenge in doing what the Lord asks us to do is actually to do it—not just to talk about it, but to *do* it. It is not good enough just to have one's name on the rolls of the Church, nor is it good enough to sit back, not participate, and expect others to do the work. We have no paid ministry, and salvation comes by each member's doing the things he has been called to do, attending the meetings, and daily living a Christlike life to the best of his ability. Salvation, exaltation, and many other spiritual and temporal blessings come to the doer of the word, and not the hearer only. May each one of us decide now to be doers of the word.

Sometimes we make the mistake of calling this church "our church." However, we did not start it, and we could not keep it from accomplishing its eternal purpose: it is the Church of Jesus Christ and the Lord leads His own church. It was begun, not by the vote of men, but by the Lord acting in the way He has always acted in such matters. He raised up a prophet and gave him the authority to act for the Lord and to receive revelation for the direction of the Lord's church. Then, step by step, the Lord revealed just exactly how His church should be organized and established.

If it is, then, the kingdom of God on the earth, if it is the Church of Jesus Christ, then it belongs to all of our Father's children who will come in at the strait and narrow gate. Let me read these words of the Lord:

> Behold, I have come unto the world to bring redemption unto the world, to save the world from sin.
>
> Therefore, whoso repenteth and cometh unto me as a little child, him will I receive, for of such is the kingdom of God. Behold, for such I have laid down my life, and have taken it up again; therefore repent, and come unto me ye ends of the earth, and be saved. (3 Nephi 9:21–22.)

Because the Lord has commanded us, we extend the invitation to all men everywhere to find out for themselves if this is not the kingdom of God on the earth, even the Church of Jesus Christ. Find out what the teachings are, ask the Lord if they are true, and see if He will not bear witness to your soul of the truth of all these things. He will give those who seek such a witness a feeling and understanding that they will not receive anyplace else outside of the Church. Those who want to know, and who will ask Him, can know. May the Lord so bless us to this end.

Revealed Religion

Living in the light of a revealed religion means that we do not have to invent the principles by which we choose to be governed. Our pattern and principles have already been established by the Lord. He then provides a way by which all men can know his law is divine and gives them their freedom to follow it.

We have just sung "Praise to the Man," a hymn written in commemoration of the Prophet Joseph Smith, whose birth date we celebrate on December 23. He was born in 1805 and was the instrument in the hands of the Lord to restore the authority, ordinances, and organization of The Church of Jesus Christ. We do not worship Joseph Smith as we do Jesus Christ, because Jesus Christ is the Son of God, the Mediator, the Atoner, the name whereby all mankind can be saved and find their way back to the presence of God.

Joseph Smith was the prophet of this last dispensation. It was the Prophet Joseph Smith who, on the banks of the Susquehanna River, received the Holy Priesthood under the inspiration of the Lord so that the authority and right to act in God's name was restored to the world once again. The Bible says that no man can take this honor unto himself, except he is called of God as was Aaron. (See Hebrews 5:4.) Aaron was called by his brother Moses, who was a prophet. (See Exodus 4:28–30.) Thus, the authority to act in God's name comes when the Lord speaks through His prophets and causes them to act in

Remarks given at a member missionary meeting in College Park, Pennsylvania, December 1975.

His name. His followers have His authority and receive that authority through His prophets.

We are grateful that such a prophet was raised up in these latter days and that through Joseph Smith the Lord first established the authority to act in the name of God, and then established the organization of the gospel of Jesus Christ. This is the Church of Jesus Christ. It is a divine organization.

What makes it different from other organizations is simply this: in an organization that is established and run by men, the direction of such an organization comes from men. Men determine what is going to happen. In the Church of Jesus Christ, the Lord provides a priesthood with Apostles and prophets who can receive revelation from God; thus, God himself can lead His own church. That's the difference between a divine organization and an organization that is established and run by men. We revere and cherish the name of the Prophet Joseph Smith, for the Lord raised him up to restore His organization and His church once again to the world.

This is not the first restoration of the gospel of Jesus Christ. If we look at the great prophets in the Old Testament and the New Testament, we see the same pattern occurring over and over again. The first, of course, was Father Adam, but eventually the people became wicked and it was necessary from time to time to raise up prophets such as Noah, Moses, Isaiah, and many others. The Lord spoke to them and restored again the same principles, church, and organization that originally existed but was lost because of the wickedness of the people. It happened again at the time of Christ; for when the Savior came, in effect to restore His own gospel, even the Church of Jesus Christ, there were a number of religious organizations in that day—such as the Sadducees, the Pharisees, and the Essenes— none of whom the Lord accepted or recognized as His true church. Therefore He systematically went about calling twelve Apostles, organizing His church, giving them the authority, appointing them to different offices and callings and establishing the Church of Jesus Christ upon the earth under His direction. And then, when He was crucified and resurrected, He left with the twelve Apostles the authority to act in His name and also provided them with the gift of the Holy Ghost, the inspiration of the Spirit, so that from His eternal throne He could continue to direct His church. The day that Jesus Christ can no longer run His church is the day that it will no longer be His church; and so in The Church of Jesus Christ of Latter-day Saints there are always Apostles and prophets who have the revelation and inspiration to lead the Lord's church in the Lord's way.

The world doesn't always understand this. They come to us and say, "Why don't you change this? Why don't you do that?" The answer is that we are powerless to change it because it is not our church. We are members of the Lord's church and He reveals to us those things we need to know to return to His presence, and those are the laws and doctrines and government of the kingdom of God. We didn't start this church. In a sense, it's not our church. Sometimes we get carried away and we say it is our church, but it is not. This is the Church of Jesus Christ. He established it when he raised up a prophet and restored the authority; and then, step by step, He restored through revelation every key for the establishment of this church.

The Prophet Joseph Smith did something else that was extremely significant. If this is the Church of Jesus Christ, there must be a way that the Lord would provide for people to learn whether it is true. And so, through the inspiration of the Spirit, the Lord led the Prophet Joseph Smith and caused him to translate plates which were the ancient record of a remnant of the House of Israel who lived on this continent centuries ago. The translation of that record has come to be known today as the Book of Mormon.

The Book of Mormon is the religious record of a great civilization and speaks of God's dealings with this people. But the Book of Mormon is something more, and the Lord Himself tells us the reason for bringing the book forward. There is indication in the Book of Mormon that He would bring forth a second witness for Jesus Christ in a day and age when the world would not be anxious to accept the Bible as the word of God; when there would be people who would say, "It is a good historical record, but no one knows if it is true"; when there would be people who would say that Jesus was a great man, but of course he could not be the Son of God; and when there would be people who would doubt the authenticity of the biblical record. In order to sustain the truths that are established in the Bible, the Lord caused a second record to be brought forward in this generation, testifying that indeed Jesus is the Christ, and the principles and teachings that are taught in the Holy Bible are verified and borne out to be true.

The Lord tells us in the Bible that by the mouths of two or more witnesses shall a thing be established (see Matthew 18:16); and so the Bible and the Book of Mormon stand as two witnesses to the world that God lives and that Jesus is the Christ, that He has not forgotten His children, that the kingdom of God is on the earth, and that there are certain principles by which all mankind must abide or there can be no salvation in His kingdom. It is clear, it is plain, and it is precious.

Some people can't understand the principles of priesthood, faith, repentance, baptism, or other doctrines we discuss. But everybody can understand a book. As a person prayerfully reads the pages of this inspired book, he will know with certainty the divine mission of Jesus Christ and that this work is true. From the final pages of the Book of Mormon, we read:

> Wherefore, nothing that is good denieth the Christ, but acknowledgeth that he is.
>
> And ye may know that he is, by the power of the Holy Ghost; wherefore I would exhort you that ye deny not the power of God; for he worketh by power, according to the faith of the children of men, the same today and tomorrow, and forever. (Moroni 10:6–7.)

In The Church of Jesus Christ of Latter-day Saints, no one has to take anyone's word that it is true. I visited last night with a woman from the press, and she asked, "To what do you attribute the growth of your church?"

I said, "A number of things come to mind. One is that it is fundamentally and basically a family religion, and people today are looking to things that they can hang on to which will strengthen their family and traditional structures." What I didn't tell her, because I didn't think she would understand and I knew she wouldn't print it, was that the Church is true—and no amount of rhetoric, explanation, or discussion can cover up something that is true. And there is a witness that the work is true and a way, if a person will read and ponder and pray, that he can find out for himself.

As it has since 1830 when the Church was organized by Joseph Smith and a few other inspired men, this same process will continue to take place in the lives of people like you and me throughout the world. That is, they will receive understanding or knowledge concerning the Church. They will read and they will ask, "Heavenly Father, is this from thee, or is someone trying to deceive me? Does this come from thee, or is it untrue?" And they will receive an understanding as they read the book, ponder it, and pray about it. Before they finish, they will know it is true.

The strength and growth of The Church of Jesus Christ of Latter-day Saints have come about because it is not really our church. It is the Lord's church, and anybody who wants to find out about its truthfulness can find out for himself. That is the power of this religion.

Now, what does a person have to do to be saved? We hear that question all over the world. Let me tell you what the Lord says. I would like to read two passages of scripture. The first happens to be from the Book of Mormon, but it is completely in harmony with and can be documented in a dozen places in the Bible as well. The two books are in harmony with each other; they both come from the same God. The Lord Jesus Christ appeared to these Book of Mormon people just as He appeared to the people in Jerusalem. He taught them, and He told them what they must do in order to be saved:

> And this is my doctrine, and it is the doctrine which the Father hath given unto me; and I bear record of the Father, and the Father beareth record of me, and the Holy Ghost beareth record of the Father and me; and I bear record that the Father commandeth all men, everywhere, to repent and believe in me.
>
> And whoso believeth in me, and is baptized, the same shall be saved; and they are they who shall inherit the kingdom of God.
>
> And whoso believeth not in me, and is not baptized, shall be damned. (3 Nephi 11:32–34.)

So important was this doctrine that the Lord talked about what needed to be done, and then He talked about the penalty if it was not done. And where is the correlation in the Bible? First of all, Jesus Christ offered Himself as the perfect example by going into the waters of baptism with John the Baptist. Why should the Savior do that if it was not necessary? "Suffer it to be so now," he explained, "to fulfil all righteousness" (Matthew 3:15). Later, when the Lord spoke to Nicodemus He said that a man must be born again of the water and of the Spirit or he cannot enter into the kingdom of God. (See John 3:5.) And then, at the end of His ministry, He told the Apostles, "Go ye into all the world, and preach the gospel to every creature. He that believeth and is baptized shall be saved; but he that believeth not shall be damned." (Mark 16:15–16.)

The principle in both records is clearly established: Entrance into the kingdom of God comes through baptism.

So important is this requirement that the Lord returns to it often as He teaches the Book of Mormon people: "And again I say unto you, ye must repent, and become as a little child, and be baptized in my name, or ye can in nowise receive these things" (3 Nephi 11:37). He adds here that to "become as a little child" is also necessary to obtain an inheritance in the kingdom of God.

In the very next verse, He once again reaffirms His initial statement: "And again I say unto you, ye must repent, and be baptized in my name, and become as a little child, or ye can in nowise inherit the kingdom of God." And then, "Verily, verily, I say unto you, that this is my doctrine, and whoso buildeth upon this buildeth upon my rock, and the gates of hell shall not prevail against them." (3 Nephi 11:38–39.)

Both records, then, say that you and I, or any of God's children, must come into His kingdom through belief in Jesus Christ and through baptism. Remember, the Lord says that not everybody will do it—not because they can't do it, but because they won't do it. He then said, "strait is the gate, and narrow is the way"—which means that there are specific things we must do to get in—"which leadeth unto life, and few there be that find it" (Matthew 7:14). His arms are open to all who would believe on Him and enter into His kingdom.

The Lord makes it clear that we need to be baptized in order to gain entrance into His kingdom; and so when we teach the gospel of Jesus Christ, we teach baptism because there is no other way. The second requirement is one that was received by the Prophet Joseph Smith regarding the celestial glory. In the

New Testament Paul spoke of the different degrees of glory (see 1 Corinthians 15:40–41), and this is expounded on by the Lord through the Prophet Joseph Smith. He explains that in the celestial or highest of these glories, "There are three heavens or degrees; And in order to obtain the highest, a man must enter into this order of the priesthood [meaning the new and everlasting covenant of marriage]; And if he does not, he cannot obtain it. He may enter into the other, but that is the end of his kingdom; he cannot have an increase." (D&C 131:1–4.)

Now, what does that mean? A number of miles from here, dedicated this last year, is the Washington Temple. The difference between this chapel or any other chapel and the Washington Temple is that in the temple ordinances are performed that will help a person progress when he leaves this life. You see, the priesthood—or authority to act in the name of God—is used on this earth to seal people together in marriage. That priesthood or authority is recognized by God, and therefore it binds people together not only in this life, but also in the next life. Remember Christ's statement to Peter, that "whatsoever thou shalt bind on earth shall be bound in heaven: and whatsoever thou shalt loose on earth shall be loosed in heaven" (Matthew 16:19). The authority to act in the name of God allows people to seal on earth, and that sealing is recognized in heaven.

What happens in the temple? Well, the principal things that happen are temple marriages. What is a temple marriage? It's much like any other marriage, except that the man and woman are married for time and eternity by those who have the authority to act in the name of God. Why is that so beautiful? Because nowhere else on the face of this earth will anyone promise you that you can have your marriage and family for eternity. The Lord is saying, "You gain entrance into my kingdom through baptism; you gain entrance into the highest degree of my kingdom through marriage in the temple." This is eternal marriage we are talking about, a marriage that enables eternal life on a family basis with our Father in Heaven. That is pretty wonderful in a world that says a marriage is performed "until death do ye part" and where no one, according to most of that world, can really tell us what will happen when we leave this earth.

The promise comes from God that if we do the things that He asks, we will inherit His kingdom. And so it is that the Church of Jesus Christ, the Lord's church, offers to the world the means by which we might return to the presence of God.

Let me speak now as a father. I have five children; the oldest is fourteen and the youngest is two. We love all our children, but it is a very normal household. I called my wife the other night (I had been gone for about a week) and I said, "How have the children been?" She replied, "Your four-year-old son went to church with his boots on, but he had no shoes in his boots. When his feet got wet, he took off his boots and went wandering around church in his stocking feet." That's Alex.

Let me tell you what the Church does for my family. In other religious organizations, you go to your minister or priest or rabbi to receive the direction of a spiritual leader. In this church, male members are given the priesthood so they can become the spiritual leaders in their own homes. In the Church, there is nothing more beautiful than for a father to be in a position so that his family can look to him—and alongside him, to Mother—for spiritual as well as temporal leadership. And the Church does that for every father who will accept the responsibility.

The Church teaches us three things, basically, in order that we might become spiritual leaders in our homes. First is family prayer. We pray together as families. It encourages us and it helps to teach us.

In our home, we hold family prayer night and morning. It is a great source of unity, strength, and peace in a world that takes all members of the family in different directions. Family prayer helps keep us together, and there is a feeling of peace when we go out into the world after taking a minute to kneel in prayer. We gather together as a family, and I will give the family prayer or call on another member of the family to do it. Then we call on each of the children to say their own personal prayers. Of course the younger ones are just learning how to pray, and so we help them a little bit. This is one of our responsibilities to our children—to help them to know how to pray; and the Church helps me to do this if I'm not quite sure how. As a result, when our oldest boys says, "I won't say my personal prayers with the family, I will say them privately,'' that's all right, because I know that by now he knows how to pray. And so the spiritual tradition of prayer is taught in our home; and when our children leave us, they will know how to pray. That's one of the things the Church does to help the father be the spiritual leader in his own home.

Second, the Church teaches us and helps us to hold what we call family home evening. We wouldn't miss ours. I'm not able to be home all the time but when I'm home, nothing interferes with home evening because we are together as a family. Sister Dunn takes the lead when I am not there. The Church publishes a family home evening resource manual, and in it are discussions and lessons which teach fundamental Christian principles in a modern world. Sister Dunn and I don't teach all of those discussions. We go to the index and select the lessons that suit our family needs. I do not do it all myself; the whole family participates and parts are assigned. We do other things in addition to having lessons. We often have activities during family home evening. The important thing is that we do it together as a family.

I guess one of our favorite family home evenings is the one we call ''open night,'' where every member of the family will have a chance to say anything he wants and the rest of the members of the family will be quiet and listen. This is particularly popular with the younger children because no one listens to them very long. We don't really start with our two-year-old, because she says anything she wants anyway. Our four-year-old is beginning to like this activity because no one stands still very long and listens to him during a busy day. He usually starts with the Three Bears and ends up with what went on with his friends that day. Everybody sits and listens—and when he's through, he knows that he belongs to this family and that we care. That's the whole purpose of this time together.

Our seven-year-old has questions and things she wants to say, as does the nine-year-old; and our oldest has some good questions, and this gives us a chance to discuss them.

Of course, you don't really know how you've done as a parent until the children have grown up. But at least we are talking with each other; we have established communication and we hope to continue that. I thank the Lord for this great program known as family home evening, which the Church has given to us as parents to help provide leadership in the home.

The third way in which the Church blesses my family is nothing more or less than priesthood quorum meetings, held every week for all men who hold the priesthood. We are instructed in the doctrines of the kingdom and in the organization of the Church, so that we are better able to teach the gospel and answer questions at home.

I am grateful to the Lord for a revealed religion that allows me to be a leader in my home and, along with my wife, be the spiritual leaders to the members of our family. In The Church of Jesus Christ of Latter-day Saints the spiritual leader is not necessarily the bishop, although he is the spiritual leader to the ward. And, unlike in other religions, the family's primary spiritual leader is not the priest, or the rabbi, or the minister. In the Church every father and mother stand in that position, and the Lord gives them help to become the spiritual leaders in their own home.

I assume that most of you are members of the Church; maybe some of you are not. If you are a visitor tonight and you are not a member of this church, we certainly welcome you. We are happy to have you with us. As I said before, sometimes we call it our church, but it is more than that. The Church is for all our Father's children, and its doctrines and teachings will help everybody. Anyone who wants to know of its truth can know; the missionaries can explain to them exactly what the Church means, what its doctrines are, and how to find out for themselves. The beauty of this church is that the Lord can let you know. So we invite you, if you will, to come and know for yourself. Come join us—not in our church, but in His church, and see if these things are not true.

Now, if you're in a family where everyone isn't a member of the Church, we suggest you try to set a good example. Let your message be your Christlike actions. Be the kind of person the Church teaches you to be, and your message will change the heart of someone you love and with whom you would like to share the gospel.

And Dad, if you're here today and you are not a member yet

while other family members are, perhaps now is the time. This church invites you to take your rightful place. Maybe now is the time to unite your family in the gospel. Don't make them wait longer.

Look into it carefully and unite your household. The Lord invites you to do this and in His name, we invite you to do this. What a blessing it is to have everybody going in the same direction.

May the Lord bless us to cherish our families and live the principles of His true gospel.

A Prophet's Story

The first vision is at the very foundation of our religion. It is our heritage. It happened in our time. It is for our generation. In a sense it is as if we were there, because the Spirit of the Lord confirms its reality to all seekers after truth.

You were born on the twenty-third of December, 1805, in the town of Sharon, Windsor County, Vermont. Your father was a farmer—a respectable farmer, but of somewhat humble circumstances. You spent the early years of your life on your father's farm, which was nestled in the rolling green hills of the state of Vermont.

When you were nearly ten years old, your family moved to what is now called Wayne County in upstate New York, where your family again pursued the occupation of farming. To help supplement the family income, you worked for other farmers nearby.

Some five years after you moved to New York, there commenced a great religious revival in your area. Crowds united themselves to different religious parties as a result of this religious fervor. At first there was unity among the different sects, but as time went on they contended against each other in hopes of winning additional converts.

You are now in your fifteenth year and your father's family, along with all of the families in the area, is approached by several religious faiths. The confusion leads you to wonder, "Which of all these parties is right?"

Address given in general conference April 1970.

While seeking an answer, you come across a passage of scrip-ture in the Bible that says, "If any of you lack wisdom, let him ask of God, that giveth to all men liberally, and upbraideth not; and it shall be given him" (James 1:5). Never did any passage of scripture come with more power to the heart of man than this does at this time to yours.

In compliance with the biblical admonition, you retire to the woods not far from your home on the morning of a beautiful, clear spring day in 1820; and you pour out your heart in prayer to your Father in Heaven.

To your astonishment, you see a pillar of light exactly over your head, above the brightness of the sun. It descends grad-ually until it falls upon you. When the light is resting on you, you see two personages, whose brightness and glory defy all description, standing above you in the air. One of them speaks, calling you by name and says, "This is My Beloved Son. Hear Him!" (Joseph Smith–History 1:17.)

You are in the presence of God the Father and His Son Jesus Christ.

As you gain your composure you ask the question as to which of all the sects you should join. You are instructed to join none of them, and you are given other instructions before the great vision closes.

A few days later you recount this vision to a minister. To your surprise he treats the whole experience not only lightly but with great contempt.

Word of the vision spreads, and you undergo great persecu-tion. A few who know you, such as the farmer for whom you work, stand by you and refer to your experience as the sweet dream of a pure-minded boy. But for the most part you undergo scathing criticism, and you are astonished that an obscure boy like you, between fourteen and fifteen years of age, could be the object of such bitter persecution—especially from men of high standing. This causes you to say in your heart, "Why persecute me for telling the truth?" (Joseph Smith–History 1:25.) You had seen a vision, you knew it, and you knew that God knew it; you could not deny it, neither dared you deny it without coming under the condemnation of God.

Nonetheless, the persecution continues.

It is on the night of September 21–22, 1823, that you are given further divine instructions in answer to your prayers. An angel appears, identifying himself as the angel Moroni. He tells you the Lord has a work for you to do, and he describes the location of golden plates that are buried in a nearby hill. You are told that these plates contain a record of God's dealings with a people that once lived and flourished on the American continent.

These gold plates are ultimately entrusted to you, and by the gift and power of God you translate them into a volume that becomes known as the Book of Mormon.

You discover that this book verifies the truths of the Bible. It establishes the reality of the death, burial, resurrection, and teachings of Jesus Christ. It spells out in detail what a man must do to gain salvation, and it offers all men a simple test to determine whether the volume is true—a test of faith, prayer, and reading.

The sacred record speaks of baptism, and it becomes evident that divine authority is necessary to carry out divine ordinances. In order for this part of the Restoration to be fulfilled, you are visited by a personage who identifies himself as John the Baptist and bestows on you the authority to baptize and perform other ordinances of the priesthood of Aaron.

Shortly after this, Peter, James, and John, angelic beings sent from God, confer on you the priesthood of Melchizedek in order that the full and complete authority to act in the name of God might be restored to the earth.

On April 6, 1830, at Fayette, Seneca County, state of New York, you organize The Church of Jesus Christ of Latter-day Saints under divine direction.

In 1830 you count six members of the Church. One year later, over two thousand members attend the second annual conference.

As the Church grows, persecution grows. You organize in New York, but persecution soon causes you to move the headquarters of the Church to Kirtland, Ohio. Finally as persecution still follows your beleaguered Saints, you push further toward the frontiers of the growing country, and the Church is moved to Missouri.

Ultimately, you direct the Saints to drain a swamp on the

Illinois side of the Mississippi River and build a city, which is to become larger than the city of Chicago. Nauvoo is its name. You enjoy peace for a time, and the worldwide missionary work goes on. Yet the storms of persecution begin to gather once again. Charges and countercharges are made. Through the evil designs of men, you have already been arrested thirty-seven times. Not once have you been convicted.

Now you are asked to come to Carthage to stand trial, but are fearful because of the ruthless, lawless nature of the mobs. Nevertheless, on June 24, 1844, you and several associates set out for Carthage. You observe that you are going like a lamb to the slaughter, but you are calm as a summer's morning.

You arrive in Carthage, and you are immediately arrested. The governor of the state promises you protection, but this does not materialize.

And now it is a hot, sultry summer afternoon, June 27, 1844.

A mob assembles and storms the jail, bursting past the jailer, firing shots through the door and window. Your brother Hyrum is shot dead in your sight, and one other person is wounded.

You spring to the window and are struck immediately by three shots. You utter your last mortal words, "Oh Lord, My God," and fall dead.

Yes, your name is Joseph Smith, Jr., prophet of the living God; and though you seal your testimony with your blood, the Church of Jesus Christ goes on.

Today millions revere you as a prophet, seer, and revelator; thousands are added to that number each year.

You restored the Church and kingdom of God under the direction of Jesus Christ. Your message concerning the Savior can be summarized best in your own words: "And now, after the many testimonies which have been given of him, this is the testimony, last of all, which we give of him: that he lives! For we saw him, even on the right hand of God; and we heard the voice bearing record that he is the Only Begotten of the Father—That by him, and through him, and of him, the worlds are and were created, and the inhabitants thereof are begotten sons and daughters unto God." (D&C 76:22–24.)

I bear my witness to you that Joseph Smith is a prophet of the living God.

I bear sacred witness that the power and ordinances of the gospel of Jesus Christ are in this church.

I bear sacred witness that a prophet of God guides the Church today.

I bear witness that the Church of Jesus Christ is led by Jesus Christ.

I know they live.

I know they live.

In the name of Jesus Christ, amen.

Index